# Whispers of God's love

## Touching the Lives of
## Loved Ones After Death

### MITCH FINLEY

### Foreword by Andrew M. Greeley

Liguori/Triumph
LIGUORI, MISSOURI

Published by Liguori/Triumph • An imprint of Liguori Publications
Liguori, Missouri • www.liguori.org

Parts of this book were originally published in 1995 under the title *Whispers of Love* by The Crossroad Publishing Company, New York, New York.

**Library of Congress Cataloging-in-Publication Data**

Finley, Mitch.
    Whispers of God's love : touching the lives of loved ones after death / Mitch Finley.—Rev. ed.
      p. cm.
    Rev. ed. of: Whispers of love. 1995.
    ISBN 0-7648-1210-6
    1. Apparitions—Case studies. I. Finley, Mitch. Whispers of love. II. Title.

BF1261.2.F55   2004
133.9—dc22
                              2004048602

All scriptural citations are taken from the *New Revised Standard Version of the Bible*, copyright 1989 by the Division of Christian Education of the National Council of the Churches of Christ in the USA. All rights reserved. Used with permission.

Printed in the United States of America
08 07 06 05 04   5 4 3 2 1
Revised edition 2004

# ACKNOWLEDGMENTS

My thanks to Peter Feuerherd who originally suggested the idea for this book. A bow to Jim Breig who was also present when the aforementioned luminary floated the idea, for letting me have it when it sounded to him, too, like a good idea for a book.

Thanks, also, to the many newspaper editors who published my letters inviting people to send me their stories.

Finally, many thanks to the people who sent their stories so that I might share them with readers. May your kindness to me, on behalf of others, return to you a hundredfold.

The lyrics quoted from John Stewart's song, "Across the Milky Way," are copyright 1992 by John Stewart. The song is on John Stewart's remarkable CD *Teresa...and the Lost Songs* (the title song is about Mother Teresa of Calcutta), available from Homecoming Records, P.O. Box 2050, Malibu, CA 90265.

*This book is dedicated to the memory
of my maternal grandparents,
Walter and Ruby (Day) Klinghammer.
Grandma died in 1968, Grandpa in 1992.
There will be a reunion.*

*If all the hearts that the Spirit loves
Were standing side by side
They would be forever long
And ten thousand miles wide.
Turn them all to stars
Across the Milky Way,
Truly they would make
The night as bright as day.*

JOHN STEWART, "ACROSS THE MILKY WAY"

# CONTENTS

# FOREWORD

I've never had one of the experiences about which Mitch Finley writes in this fascinating book. Worse luck for me, perhaps, I am the least psychically sensitive of humans—surely not among those whom the Irish call "the Dark Ones."

In my study of the sociology of mystical and parapsychological experiences which Mr. Finley is good enough to cite, I was asking perfectly valid sociological questions about the incidence and prevalence of such experiences. I was not attempting to "prove" that in such experiences one is in fact in real contact with the dead, much less that there is life after death—issues which go far beyond the professional competence of empirical social science. The ridicule that my research occasioned—and still occasions—suggests to me that dogmas are as common in science as they are in religion.

A colleague from another country did an elaborate study of more than two hundred such experiences. Though he offered it for publication at the time that books on NDE (Near Death Experiences) were very popular, not a single New York publishing company was interested. Even the lure of a possible bestseller could not break through the hard shell of agnosticism.

I find the passing of this resistance strange. An experience that is obviously widespread in our society is either ignored or dismissed as "wish fulfillment." Obviously people wish they could contact their dead. But it does not follow, save as priori dogma, that their experiences are no more than elaborate self-deceptions. As William James observed in *The Variety of Religious Experiences*, those who have had such experiences will not give them up and those who reject such experiences have no right to exclude them on apriori grounds.

Do the incidents recorded in this book (and in my research) prove anything? I like the reply of Professor Carol Zaleski that they are not proof of anything, but only signs—signs at a minimum that we live in a mysterious, surprising, and always wonderful universe.

For those like myself who have never been there, Zaleski's view is the only way to approach the mysterious, wonderful, and surprising stories in this book. For those who have no proof is necessary.

ANDREW GREELEY
FIFTEENTH SUNDAY IN ORDINARY TIME
2004

# INTRODUCTION

That life—though not life as we know it—continues on the other side of death is a conviction shared by various religions and philosophies, from Christians of various stripes to devotees of Eastern religions. Death is a transition from life in time and space to "eternal" life. Note, however, that "eternal" is not itself the same as "endless time." Eternity is a unique mode of being entirely, one that we begin to experience even in time and space. Jesus, in the Gospel of John, says: "This is eternal life, that they may know you, the only true God, and Jesus Christ whom you have sent" (17:3). Essentially, then, eternal life is an intimate union with God or the Divine Mystery Christians know as Love, an intimacy which begins here and now and is completed on the other side of natural death.

It's not as odd as it may sound, then, to suggest that those who have died may, on an unpredictable basis, manifest themselves to loved ones still plodding through history. Indeed, if love transcends time and space yet is present *in* time and space, there is no reason why deceased loved ones may not, on occasion, be present to and communicate in some way with those still living in historical time. Researchers, in fact, have turned up evidence that many people do experience contact, in various ways, with deceased loved ones.

Experiences of the personal presence of deceased relatives and/ or friends, are more common than one might think. In 1984, 1988, and 1989, in its General Social Survey, the University of Chicago's National Opinion Research Center (NORC) asked a representative sampling of the U. S. population: "How often have you felt as though you were really in touch with someone who died?" Affirmative responses came from 42 percent of those asked who were not widowed and 53 percent of those widowed. Among teenagers, 38 percent reported being in touch with someone who died. (See *Religion As Poetry* by Andrew M. Greeley [Transaction Publishers, 1995], especially Chapter 12, "Religious Stories and Contact With the Dead.")

Louis E. LaGrand, Ph.D., is Distinguished Service Professor Emeritus at the State University of New York College at Potsdam and Adjunct Professor for Health Careers at the Eastern Campus of Suffolk Community College. He is also a founder and past president of the board of directors of Hospice of St. Lawrence Valley, Inc., among many other distinctions. In his book *Messages and Miracles: Extraordinary Experiences of the Bereaved* (Llewellyn Publications, 1999), Professor LaGrand says:

> The realization that apparitions of the deceased…have been consistently interacting with the living is one of the little publicized hallmarks of human history. However, the experience is not new to the bereaved, nor is it rare for a selected number of people who are not mourning the death of a loved one.

Based on his research, Professor LaGrand suggests six reasons that deceased loved ones "visit" following their death:

1. To provide comfort and reassurance.
2. To assist those who are themselves dying.
3. To finish unfinished business.
4. To suggest ways to solve problems.
5. To emphasize that love is eternal.
6. To protect by helping a bereaved person avoid a potentially harmful situation before it happens.

Mind you, we're not talking about an experience similar to Ebenezer Scrooge's visit with the ghost of Jacob Marley in Charles Dickens' *A Christmas Carol*. The experiences of real people are never as wild and dramatic as that. Sometimes, however, what happens to real people has a similar effect. They become less fearful, more at peace with their lives.

The reader may ask: Are those who report encounters with deceased loved ones perhaps a couple of fries short of a Happy Meal? On the contrary, if anything they are often reluctant to tell their story, not wanting to be thought peculiar. In fact, there are famous people whose sanity is beyond question who reported such experiences. Stories from some of these appear at the beginning of the section following this introduction.

Theologically, the accounts in this book fit into the ancient Christian doctrine of the communion of saints. This doctrine is quite simple. It merely states that a real and spiritual union exists among the entire community of those who believe in Christ, living and dead. We're all in this together, both those in time, on earth, and those in eternity, and we can help one another through our prayers. Believers in the Roman Catholic, Eastern Orthodox, and—to a lesser degree—Anglican communities believe that we may cultivate a continuing intimacy with friends and relatives who have gone before us into the mystery we call "eternal life" or "heaven."

About half the population, apparently, does not experience the presence of a deceased loved one, so we can't say that this experience is universal or an everyday, ordinary phenomenon. Commenting on the NORC findings, sociologist Andrew M. Greeley wrote: "Those who believe in life after death, who pray frequently and who regard God more as a lover than a judge" are more likely to have encounters with deceased loved ones. Clearly, such experiences happen frequently enough to make them worth attending to. Those who share them here do so because they want others to benefit from their experiences, as well.

The title of this book comes from a hymn, "Blessed Assurance," written in the late nineteenth century by Phoebe P. Knapp and Fanny Crosby. During the months I worked on this book, I thought *Blessed Assurance* would make a good title. But as I read more and more stories and pondered their meaning, and as I reflected upon the lyrics of the old hymn, gradually I concluded that the present title, based on lyrics from the same song, was more appropriate. The hymn praises God for "echoes of mercy, whispers of love." This phrase describes perfectly what people feel when they encounter the presence of a deceased relative or friend. Invariably, the experience is a loving and healing one.

What are we—those of us who have not had such encounters with deceased loved ones—to make of the accounts given here? There can be no absolutely convincing scientific proof of anything, of course, only conclusions drawn from faith, love, and personal experience. But if we believe that the essence of the human person survives natural death, then we may draw from stories such as these some hope and courage for ourselves and those we love.

As I wrote this book, I found myself reflecting on the unique meaning of each story. Before long, I decided to include my own thoughts in the hope that they will help, in some small degree, to connect the stories to the everyday real world that we live in. I suggest that you, kind reader, pursue similar meditations of your own.

The last thing I wish to encourage is a preoccupation with eternity or "the afterlife." Let the afterlife take care of itself, I say. Our task, for now, is to focus on *this* life, to live it to the hilt—the joy, the sorrow, and the vast expanses of ambiguity in-between. Indeed, that seems clearly to be the focus even of those who "return" from the eternal realm to comfort and encourage loved ones still on their earthly journey.

Read these stories and these reflections, then, in the spirit in which they were written, a spirit of kindness, realism, generosity and good will. Perhaps you will gain from them the gift that they offer—a renewed sense of faith, hope, and love; a deeper conviction that this life is worth living today and forever; and a calm, uncomplicated belief that when this life draws to its natural close what awaits us is not oblivion or punishment but life in its fullness—a life beyond anything we can begin to imagine or hope for, but a life which we do catch glimpses of in our love and care for one another in this present existence.

## *Thomas Merton and the Spirit of His Father*

Thomas Merton, the famous Trappist monk and author who died in 1968, wrote a decade or so after the fact about sensing, as an adolescent, the presence of his deceased father. In his famous autobiography, *The Seven Storey Mountain*, Merton recalled:

> I was in my room. It was night. The light was on. Suddenly it seemed to me that Father, who had now been dead more than a year, was there with me. The sense of his presence was as vivid and as real and as startling as if he had touched my arm or spoken to me. The whole thing passed in a flash...

# Reflection

### "Presence" May or May Not Be Visual

*When loved ones who have died*
*do "return"*
*their presence comes about in various ways.*
*The way they return seems to be determined*
*more by us than by them.*
*Some people actually see*
*the deceased loved one.*
*Other times, there is more a sense of*
*a powerful, invisible, but undoubtedly real*
*"presence" that has no visual component.*
*People who are of a more intellectual bent*
*such as Thomas Merton*
*seem to have experiences that include*
*no visual "sighting"*
*of the deceased person.*
*Regardless, however,*
*the experience is no less real.*

## Frederick Buechner Receives
## a *"Visit"* From an Old Friend

Frederick Buechner, Presbyterian minister and bestselling author, reported his experience in a talk he gave in 1987, sponsored by the Book-of-the-Month Club, which appeared later in *Spiritual Quests: The Art and Craft of Religious Writing,* edited by William Zinsser (Houghton Mifflin, 1988). Buechner told his audience that a good friend had died one year previously, and a couple of months later he and his wife stayed overnight with the man's widow. That night, he dreamed that his friend stood there in the guest room "looking very much the way he always did in the navy blue jersey and white slacks that he often wore..."

Frederick Buechner told his friend how much they missed him and how happy he was to see him, and his friend acknowledged this. "Then I said, 'Are you really there, Dudley?' I meant was he there in fact and truth, or was I merely dreaming that he was? His answer was that he was really there. And then I said, 'Can you prove it?' 'Of course,' he said. Then he plucked a strand of blue wool out of his jersey and tossed it to me, and I caught it between my index finger and my thumb, and the feel of it was so palpable and so real that it woke me up. That's all there was to the dream."

It seemed, Buechner said, as if his friend came to do what he did, and then he left. The next morning at breakfast, Buechner described his dream, and he had barely finished when his wife spoke. She declared that she had seen a strand of blue wool on the guest room carpet that morning as she was getting dressed, and "she was sure it hadn't been there the night before."

Buechner wondered if he was losing his mind. "I rushed upstairs to see," he told his audience, "and there it was—a little tangle of navy blue wool that I have in my wallet as I stand here today."

# Reflection

### Believing and Knowing

*No matter how a friend or relative may*
*communicate with us after death,*
*the purpose seems always to be the same.*
*They want to reassure and comfort us,*
*and when they do*
*they are always still their own unique selves.*
*Their unique personalities remain the same,*
*and even their sense of humor remains the same.*
*Skeptics can always find ways to discount*
*reports such as this one, of course.*
*But for those who have these experiences*
*there is no need to prove anything to anyone.*
*They don't believe anything.*
*Rather, they know something.*

## C. S. Lewis's "Chuckle in the Darkness"

The third and final example is from the famous little volume by C. S. Lewis, *A Grief Observed*. Lewis, who died in 1963, wrote about dealing with the death of his beloved wife, Joy. Facing the darkness and uncertainty with which his wife's death confronted him, Lewis described an "impression" he received "more than once" which he could only describe "by saying that it's like the sound of a chuckle in the darkness. The sense that some shattering and disarming simplicity is the real answer."

The day following an experience he simply could not dismiss, Lewis wrote: "It's the *quality* of last night's experience…that makes it worth putting down. It was quite incredibly unemotional. Just the impression of her *mind* momentarily facing my own. Mind, not 'soul' as we tend to think of soul. Certainly the reverse of what is called 'soulful.' Not at all like a rapturous reunion of lovers. Much more like getting a telephone call…from her about some practical arrangement."

Lewis said there was no "message," just "intelligence and attention." There was no sense of joy or sorrow. Neither did he feel love, in the usual sense. Nor did he feel "un-love." Lewis said that he had never imagined "the dead as being so—well, so business-like. Yet there was an extreme and cheerful intimacy. An intimacy that had not passed through the senses or the emotions at all."

# Reflection

## Worry Not

*C. S. Lewis's image of*
*"a chuckle in the darkness"*
*is one of the most delightful*
*and revealing images*
*anyone has ever come up with*
*to describe what it's like*
*when a deceased loved one*
*communicates with someone still*
*in time and space.*
*Regardless of what the experience*
*may be like in its details,*
*for many the experience is one of*
*getting a message*
*"from out of nowhere"*
*that there is nothing,*
*nothing, nothing at all*
*to be worried about.*
*Nothing at all.*

# The Encounters

# FRIENDSHIP FOR MORE
# THAN A LIFETIME

Sometimes we develop friendships when we are young that last for a lifetime. Such was the case with Victoria and Patty who were dear friends from high school days on.

Some years ago, Victoria said, "I received the news that Patty had cancer, but when I phoned her she assured me that everything would be fine due to an upcoming surgery."

Victoria listened to her friend and offered reassurance herself, but when she hung up she wished she had told Patty how dear a friend she was. "I wished I had thanked her for being there when I needed someone. I didn't because I felt that I would speak with her again."

As sometimes happens, however, Patty did not survive her struggle with cancer. She died on her birthday, February 24, 1984. Victoria recalled that when she heard the news of her friend's death she was "sick with grief." She wished with all her heart that she had told Patty what a good friend she had been. She longed for a chance to visit with her friend just one more time to recall their high school days and share one more time all the memories they cherished. Worst of all, Victoria had never been able to see Patty again, to give her a hug and say goodbye.

Much to Victoria's astonishment, however, she did indeed get to say goodbye to Patty and tell her how much she cared for her…in her dreams.

Days, weeks, months and years went by, the calendar pages fell like leaves in autumn, and for five years after Patty's death whenever Victoria needed help with some difficulty Patty came to be with her friend. "Patty would come to me in a dream," Victoria said, "and sit on the end of my bed and help me work things out. It was wonderful to have these 'visits' with Patty."

Eventually, the time came when it was no longer necessary for Patty to help her friend. The last time she appeared to Victoria in a dream she explained that she would no longer come to visit. In this dream, Victoria told Patty everything she wished she had told her before she died, and she was able, at long last, to say goodbye. "I miss these 'visits,'" Victoria commented. "She was a wonderful lady."

This was not the only time Victoria received the comfort and reassurance of visits from people she cared for who had died. In the summer of 1993, a man who worked for Victoria had a heart attack on the job, and Victoria rushed to try and revive him. "I could tell that Fred was already dead, but I tried anyway," she said.

That night, Victoria dreamed that Fred knocked on her door, and went to answer the knock. There stood Fred in the doorway. He said that he had simply come by to say thank you. I asked, "For what?" Fred just stood there and said, "For caring. Thanks for caring."

Not one to take herself too seriously, Victoria said that she woke up expecting Rod Serling, of the old "Twilight Zone" television series, to be in her living room. Still, she believes that such "visits" from deceased friends happen for a reason. Victoria had a twin sister who died as a toddler. "After all these years, at age 33, I still feel her presence," she said.

## Reflection

**Friendship Forever**

*Not everyone has true friends.*
*If we're fortunate,*
*in the course of a lifetime*
*we have a few very close friends,*
*"soul-mates," if you will,*
*a few people with whom we can open our heart*
*and be completely honest.*
*A friend is someone we can be our true self with,*
*a person with whom we can share our deepest joys and sorrows,*
*one who can listen and accept*
*and never judge or condemn.*

Saint Francis de Sales, who lived in late sixteenth- and early seventh-century Europe, wrote:

*"Friendship begun in this world*
*will be taken up again,*
*never to be broken off."*
*The love that characterizes friendship,*
*like every form of love,*
*has connections between time and eternity,*
*between this world and the next.*

# A BROTHER RETURNS
# TO GIVE REASSURANCE

Dan's brother died, and that evening he and his wife decided to spend the night at the home of Dan's parents to be nearby should they be needed. "We made up the living-room sofa," Dan said, "and turned in after everyone else."

During the night, Dan's wife awakened him. "She was shivering. I asked her what the problem was, and she told me that she had just seen my dead brother. I immediately felt one of those currents that run through your body. She said that something had caused her to wake up, and when she sat up she saw him standing across the room. He was just standing there, she explained. He said nothing, but he seemed to be at peace, as if he were telling her that he was okay. That everything was okay. I looked around, but I saw nothing, yet the electricity of the moment lingered. We talked for a while, and then we went back to sleep....

"For my part, I have never questioned the possibility that my brother really did return that night. It would have been just like him to do that as a way of putting everyone's mind at rest...."

# Reflection

**No Limits to Love**

*Do those who precede us in death*
*have any concern for us and our feelings?*
*Evidence such as this account clearly suggests*
*that they do, indeed, continue to care for us*
*and they don't want us to be concerned or worried*
*about them.*
*In other words, those who slip through the veil*
*between this life and the next*
*continue to love us just as*
*we continue to love them.*
*In other words,*
*love knows no limits, not even*
*the limits of time and space:*
*not one love for one another,*
*and not God's love for us.*

# A FATHER VISITS

Like most people, as a child Catherine experienced death only at a distance. Grandparents died, as did aunts, uncles, and friends of her family, but they were always older people or people she was not particularly close to. Then, however, Catherine's own father died, and that was different. "We shared a very close relationship," the mother of twelve children explained.

For years, Catherine's father had to cope with serious health problems—arteriosclerosis, heart attacks, open-heart surgery, a stroke, and the amputation of a leg. So all along Catherine expected that her father would not have a long life. Still, when he did die it was a very difficult time for Catherine.

Three days before Christmas, Catherine's father had a stroke and was hospitalized in a coma until January 16. "We were told that he didn't know what was going on and that all he did was simply reflexes, but I know different," Catherine said.

Following her father's death, Catherine took charge. As the oldest of five children in her family, she kept everyone on course. She got everyone to the hospital to say goodbye, directed the arrangements for the funeral and burial, and held up well. There was much to be done in the days before the funeral and through the funeral itself, and Catherine maintained...until it was time to leave the cemetery, and then grief overcame her.

Catherine said to God many nights as she lay in bed that if she could know that her father was okay, she would be okay, too. About ten days after her father's death, Catherine dreamed that she was washing dishes in her mother's kitchen. She heard the back door open, and she turned to find her father standing there.

"I remember being shocked and that my face reflected that," Catherine recalled. All she could say was, "Dad," but her father spoke saying that he couldn't stay. He had only come to tell Catherine how happy he was. It was so beautiful where he was now that Catherine couldn't begin to imagine it.

"He looked so healthy," Catherine said, "sort of glowing and at peace with no pain showing on his face for the first time I could remember. And he had both legs!"

Catherine said that her father looked no younger than his age of fifty-eight, yet he didn't look old, either, as he had when he died. Later, Catherine's oldest son who had a very close relationship with his grandfather, said that he had spoken to and seen Catherine's father after his death.

Yet another time Catherine was comforted in a dream about the death of a loved one. Her first grandchild, a boy, died of Sudden Infant Death Syndrome just two days shy of being six weeks old. "He had just been baptized the weekend before," Catherine said. The baby's father—Catherine's oldest son—and mother were visiting with the baby at the time. "Our daughter-in-law found him, and for weeks we all worried about whether he had suffered because we knew so little about Sudden Infant Death Syndrome."

Not long after her infant grandson's death, Catherine said, "I guess I had a vision of how he left us and went home."

Catherine saw the baby sleeping in his crib, as he had been when he died, and he heard a voice call him. The baby looked up, his face all smiles. A bright light was in front of him, and he turned and looked at his Mom and Dad in bed asleep. Then he stood up and ran toward the bright light. "I didn't talk to him," Catherine recalled, "or experience his presence as I had my dad's, but I knew he left peacefully and never suffered at all."

Sometimes when she is in church, Catherine hears a hymn that was sung at her father's funeral. "When that happens, I swear I can hear him say, 'Hello!' or 'Merry Christmas, Babe!'"

# Reflection

**All Lives Are Short**

*The death of a father*
*at too young an age,*
*it seems.*
*The death of a baby,*
*barely off to a good start*
*in this world*
*—deprived of so much,*
*it seems,*
*so much joy he could have brought to his family.*
*The death of a father,*
*too young,*
*and the death of a baby,*
*seem to make no sense at all,*
*and our feelings of grief are understandable.*
*But death in such cases*
*reminds us of something, too,*
*that in a way it doesn't matter*
*how long or short a life is.*
*It reminds us that for everyone*

*life is short,*
*and life,*
*no matter how many years we have,*
*finds its fulfillment in a mystery,*
*the mystery of death*
*—which is part of life*
*—on the other side of which is,*
*we believe,*
*inexpressible peace,*
*the fulfillment of all our longing:*
*"What no eye has seen,*
*nor ear heard,*
*nor the human heart conceived,*
*what God has prepared for those who love him...."*

1 CORINTHIANS 2:9

# "I KNEW I'D ONLY HAVE HIM FOR A YEAR"

Leah's first son, Jamie, was born in the days when it was standard medical procedure to give women an anesthetic to render them unconscious while giving birth, so she didn't see her baby right away. In fact, she didn't get to see him until late the second day after he was born. The nurses told her this was because the baby had an excess of mucus so they didn't want to take him from the nursery yet.

The truth was that Jamie had been born with "club feet," and the medical personnel were afraid Leah wouldn't take this news well. They didn't want a hysterical mother on their hands. "They needn't have worried," Leah said. "I was so young and ignorant that I didn't realize how serious it was until years later."

When a nurse finally brought Leah her baby, she held him and loved him as any new mother will hold and love her baby. At the same time, Leah had a premonition. "I knew I would only have him for a year. It wasn't a voice or a picture in my mind. It was just something I knew, a fact."

As the days, weeks, and months passed, the one year time limit stayed in Leah's mind. Because of the congenital deformity of his feet, Jamie spent two months in a Shriner's Hospital. After that, he had casts on his legs until he was about six months old. Then he had to wear orthopedic shoes and braces. Still, through it all the baby was a delight, "always laughing and happy," Leah said. She was fascinated by him and loved to watch him grow and develop, finding it impossible to stay away from him. "He was never left with a baby sitter."

Then, on an ordinary Wednesday, Jamie developed a fever, and by Friday he had died. "So fast, so abrupt, so final," Leah said. "He was thirteen months old."

A month after Jamie's death, Lean was visiting with her in-laws, and she was having a difficult time. She kept reliving the last day of her infant son's life. A woman who was a friend of Leah's in-laws was also visiting, and she asked if the baby had been baptized. Leah responded, "No." "Oh, how sad," the woman said, horrified. "Now he'll never see God."

Such crass insensitivity is difficult to imagine, and while at one time such theology was not uncommon, it's impossible to imagine anyone believing such a thing today. Leah was overcome with grief. "I couldn't control myself," she recalled. "I burst into tears and ran away. It was all my fault, because of me my innocent little boy couldn't be with God."

Plagued with guilt, Leah felt intense mental and emotional pain. "It was pure agony," she said. "I even prayed for insanity. I thought that would shut my mind up."

Sometimes, however, it's amazing what can trigger healing. Not many days later, Leah was driving in her car when she heard a song come on the radio. "He's got the whole world in His hands," the voice sang. Still, Leah wasn't really listening, not until the singer got to the line, "He's got the little bitty babies, in His hands, He's got the little bitty babies...."

"It was almost as if the volume had been turned up," Leah

said. "I didn't miss a word. Then I knew that the woman was wrong. I knew my little boy would see God."

Although healing had begun, Leah still hadn't found complete peace of mind and heart. Time passed, and time heals, but the hurt never went away. Leah's husband was drafted into the army, and they had another little boy, Eric, who was born two-and-one-half years, to the day, after her first child was born. A new baby brought joy, but in the back of her mind Leah could never forget her first child, Jamie. "I kept wondering what he'd think, being replaced by another baby. Would he resent it, would he think I'd forgotten him? Thoughts like these were always with me."

When Eric was a little more than a year old, Leah's husband was able to go on leave from the army, so the little family went to visit his parents. As it happened, Leah's in-laws lived not far from the cemetery where her first child was buried. "From the first day we were there," Leah said, "I had an overpowering need to take Eric to the cemetery so his brother could see him."

The cemetery Leah and Eric entered was a typical small-town cemetery, a narrow road entering through a front gate, then curving left to exit through a side gate. The moment mother and son walked through the cemetery's front gate, Eric ran ahead so fast his mother couldn't keep up with him. Up the road he ran as fast as his little legs could carry him, then he angled off into the grave sites. Finally, in the second row of graves from the road, Leah caught up with Eric. The little boy squatted over a small gravestone with the figure of an angel carved into its face. He patted the stone with his little hand, saying, "Baby? Baby?" To Leah's astonishment, Eric had run directly to his brother's grave.

"A chill went through me," Leah remembered, "and I had to sit down. Then I was filled with a warm feeling, and I knew that my little Jamie had called us so that we could all be at peace. I knew this in the same way that I had known I wouldn't have Jamie for very long. I knew he was saying goodbye and that everything was all right."

Leah has never forgotten the day she took her son, Eric, to the cemetery. He had never been to the cemetery before, he hadn't even been walking for long. Although surrounded by upright grave-stones with lambs and angels on them, Eric ran to a small, flat marker that could not be seen from the road.

"For myself," Leah said, "I need no explanation. I knew my beloved little boy was at peace and I could be at peace, too."

# Reflection

### Each Life Is a Gift

*The death of a child*
*carries a special poignancy,*
*a special sadness.*
*At the same time,*
*it sheds light on the meaning of life.*
*No matter how long,*
*no matter how brief,*
*any life has meaning*
*simply because it's a life.*
*Any life is worth celebrating*
*for what that life brings into the world*
*and into other human lives.*
*Each life is a gift,*
*and once that life has been shared with us*
*it's a life that will always be there,*
*will always be a part of the lives*
*of those who knew and loved him or her.*
*Thomas Carlyle,*
*the great nineteenth century English writer, said:*
*"One life, a little gleam of time between two eternities."*
*No matter how brief each "little gleam of time,"*
*it has an eternal impact on those around it.*
*Each life, no matter how brief, is*
*—to borrow an old advertising slogan—*
*a gift that keeps on giving.*

# GRANDMA COMES TO THE RESCUE

Only parents who have cared for babies day in, day out, week after week, month after month, year after year, really understand the extent to which parents give and give, sometimes to the point of complete exhaustion. In Kathy's case, she asked for—and received—a little relief from an unusual source.

When her fourth child, Emily, was six months old, Kathy woke from a deep sleep one night at about 2 A.M. and heard the baby crying. Kathy was so completely worn out, so in need of sleep that she couldn't drag herself out of bed, and she began to cry herself. "I felt totally exhausted and overwhelmed," she said. "I had not had a full night's sleep since the baby had been born."

Tears in her eyes and trickling down her cheeks onto her pillow, Kathy thought of her grandmother who had died ten years ago. "I asked her to please just take over for a bit," Kathy said. "Within a few minutes, Emily was asleep and she slept all night! I actually felt Gramma's presence as she soothed the baby and rocked her to sleep."

## Reflection

### A Grandparent's Love Is Unique

Arthur Kornhaber, M.D., and Kenneth L. Woodward, in *Grandparents and Grandchildren: The Vital Connection*, wrote:

> "Every time a child is born, a grandparent is born too. Society records the child's birth, and its parents, but not its grandparents."

*When we become grandparents*
*we jump into a new role,*
*we become somebody's grandmother or grandfather.*
*You may have seen a bumper sticker that proclaims:*

*Joy Is Being a Grandparent, or*
*Ask Me About My Grandchildren.*
*Grandparents smile and say*
*that grandchildren are wonderful*
*because you can enjoy them all you want,*
*but then you can give them back*
*to their parents*
*and return to the peace and quiet*
*of your own life.*
*But look around.*
*Many grandparents today*
*become supplemental parents.*
*Grandparents pick up their grandchildren*
*after school*
*and take them home*
*until their parents get off work.*
*Many grandparents today*
*end up, in effect, starting over,*
*when an unmarried daughter has a baby.*
*Life for grandparents today*
*isn't as simple as it may have been in the past.*
*All the same,*
*grandparents have special feelings*
*for their grandchildren, and those feelings*
*remain*
*when a grandparent dies.*
*The grandparent-grandchild relationship*
*remains,*
*transcending the infinitesimal distance*
*between where/when they are*
*and where/when we are.*
*We can talk with deceased grandparents,*
*and who knows what that may lead to*
*—some help with a fussy baby at night,*
*perhaps.*
*The love of a grandparent remains.*

# A TRANSCENDENT MOMENT OF GREAT HOPE

Sara had a vivid experience of the presence of her deceased mother on a cold winter's morning, and being of a poetic bent she wrote a poem about it. "This was a moment of great hope for me in a long, pain-filled winter," Sara said. Here is her poem:

### River Gift

*Seven swans a-swimming*
*startle me as I pause, pain-filled,*
*at the breakfast room window.*
*How regally they float toward the shore,*
*gliding through the glassy Potomac*
*on a shining December morning,*
*in the fourth year after my mother's death.*

*How she cherished all birds!*
*The raucous mocker, flitting chickadee,*
*drab wren, red robin and tufted titmouse—*
*every manner of wing and feather and song.*
*I wonder if she might have sent the swans*
*as a bright gift of beauty and comfort*
*to help me with the relentless pain*
*that radiates through my back.*

*I think about the communion of saints*
*and how our loved ones stay connected,*
*touching our lives despite death and its separation.*
*Dreaming at night, I have hoped for a glimpse*
*of the mother I loved so dearly.*
*She shuns my dreams somehow,*
*but then comes gliding toward me*
*With seven swimming swans*
*on a bright and cold December day.*

# Reflection

## Other Ways of Seeing

Sergius Bulgakov, a mid-twentieth-century Russian Orthodox author, offered the most remarkable observation. He said:

*"In God and in his Church*
*there is no difference*
*between living and dead,*
*and all are one*
*in the love of the Father.*
*Even the generations yet to be born*
*are part of this one*
*divine humanity."*
*We may cling to such a thought*
*with surprise and delight.*
*Imagine.*
*Yet our bodily eyes,*
*for all their blessings,*
*can't see beyond*
*the people, places, and things*
*in our path.*
*Our bodily eyes see only what's solid,*
*what's made up of atoms.*
*(Of course, at the heart of an atom*
*is the most astonishing invisibility.)*
*Our bodily eyes see only*
*what our senses can perceive.*
*But we have other forms of vision,*
*ways of seeing into the invisible realm*
*at the core of the atom,*
*where divine love*
*quietly explodes eternally.*
*And when we look with the eyes of the soul*
*we may see the most astonishing sights.*

*When we look with the eyes of the soul,*
*someone we love,*
*someone who no longer needs*
*the atoms of bodily existence*
*may come gliding toward us,*
*"With seven swimming swans*
*on a bright and cold December day."*

# THE SCENT OF
# FLOWERS NOT THERE

Joseph's five-year-old daughter died, a victim of leukemia. Not long after this, Joseph and his oldest daughter, age twelve, attended Mass at their parish church on a weekday morning. Naturally, their thoughts and prayers were focused on the little girl they both had loved so much.

After Mass, father and daughter walked slowly out of the church, and as they opened the church door to go outside, they were both overwhelmed by the beautiful but almost overpowering scent of flowers. It was springtime, but still too early for flowers. Still, Joseph and his daughter looked around for the flowers they could smell so plainly. "The scent was so overwhelming," Joseph said, "that both myself and my daughter stopped in our tracks. Thinking back, I remember that the scent lasted from two to five minutes."

Joseph and his daughter searched inside and outside the church. Perhaps a florist had brought some flowers for something going on later in the day? They even looked around the immediate neighborhood, walking about, peering here and there, stooping to look among shrubs and trees. No flowers anywhere, so finally they gave up.

"We both had a beautiful feeling of love and peace," Joseph said, "as if our deceased girl was telling us everything was just fine and to leave it all in God's hands."

Years later, Joseph drove his eighty-seven-year-old mother from Long Island, New York, to Orlando, Florida, to visit her daughter. Joseph and his family then drove off to do some sight-seeing around the state. A few weeks later, Joseph and his family returned to find his mother not feeling well at all. Joseph knew she was sick when she didn't want to go to church on Ash Wednesday, something unheard of for her.

Joseph's mother died and, as happens sometimes in families—being the contrary conglomerations that they are—Joseph and his brother disagreed about the details of their mother's funeral and burial. The conflict was intensified by the fact that Joseph has trouble hearing and must wear two hearing aids. This meant that most of the communication between he and his brother, by telephone, had to be done through Joseph's wife, which put her in the middle.

"My brother and I love each other dearly," Joseph explained, "but this was a bad situation."

Worn out from all the haggling, Joseph went down to the beach on the gulf shore and had himself "a good cry." As he cried, Joseph talked to his deceased mother, telling her all that had been happening and how he was feeling about it. "Lo and behold," he said, "my mother came to me as plain as if she were here talking to me right at this moment. What she said to me was so reassuring that all the bitterness and hatred of the time passed completely away."

The next morning, Joseph attended Mass and received the sacrament of reconciliation from the young priest who was there. "The sermon seemed to be directed right at me," he said, "and the amazing thing was that I could hear 95 percent of what he said, even though I have a hearing problem. I know in my heart that God spoke to me through my mother, the young priest, and my brother, and I was comforted and healed so that I get along as if the incident never happened."

# Reflection

### Love Goes Beyond

*A newspaper reported*
*that an unethical mortician was in jail awaiting trial.*
*Police found that the mortician*
*had more than forty bodies of deceased persons,*
*"derelicts," he called them,*
*stored in a walk-in refrigeration room.*
*All had been embalmed*
*but none were scheduled for burial.*
*"Why should I bother?" the mortician said.*
*"No one cares about these people,*
*and the city won't pay me enough to bury them*
*to cover my costs."*
*Forty people who died with no one to care*
*whether they lived or died.*
*Forty people, you see,*
*who were not loved and, perhaps,*
*loved no one.*
*You have to wonder,*
*you have to speculate*
*with a heavy heart:*
*How long before these more than forty people died*
*did they die?*
*John Henry Newman,*
*nineteenth-century English Catholic theologian, said:*
*"Fear not that your life*
*shall come to an end,*
*but rather*
*that it shall never have a beginning."*
*Fortunately,*
*most people die with someone to care,*
*and the love between people*
*remains,*

*it continues to exist,*
*it goes on having the impact*
*that only love can have*
*—healing, forgiving, comforting*
*—if we are open to it and believe.*

# Just Calling to Say "Hi"

Scott worked in the oil fields around Evanston, Wyoming, for a long time, then he did construction work in Nevada. His mother, Danny, gave him the dickens once because he never called her, and whenever she called he was never home. Since Scott was not much of a letter writer, this meant that mother and son rarely had a chance to talk. Scott replied that with his odd, long working hours the only time he could call his mother would still be asleep. Danny said that was okay with her, she could always go back to bed.

"From then on," Danny said, "he called about once a month around 4 A.M. just as he was leaving for work."

Scott died, and from then on Danny said, she would "hear" the phone ring about four o'clock in the morning. She would sit up in bed, waiting for the second ring which never came. "I would then lay awake praying for him. Was he calling me to let me know he needed my prayers?"

Later that morning, as Danny attended Mass, the congregation sang a song, "On Eagle's Wings," by Michael Joncas, which is based on Psalm 91. The song's refrain is in the third person: "And he will raise you up on eagle's wings, bear you on the breath of dawn, make you to shine like the sun, and hold you in the palm of his hand." But in Danny's mind the words echoed in the first person: "And I will raise you up...I will hold you in the palm of my hand."

"After about the third time," Danny said, "I started crying as I truly believed the significance of what was going through my mind was that God was telling me that he had taken Scott to heaven. I have not "heard" the phone ring early in the morning since that day."

# Reflection

### Allowing Ourselves to Look

*Charles, Prince of Wales*
*and heir apparent to the throne of England,*
*was presented to a beautiful American actress*
*who wore an extremely low-cut dress.*
*Without a bit of embarrassment,*
*the prince greeted the actress:*
*"Father told me*
*that if I ever met a lady*
*in a dress like yours,*
*I must look her straight in the eyes."*
*Sometimes we adopt a similar tactic*
*when someone close to us dies.*
*We avoid the startling reality before us,*
*looking instead at something else to distract us*
*so we won't be embarrassed*
*or surprised,*
*or delighted by something we didn't expect.*
*We are so shocked by death*
*that we don't want to look at it for long.*
*We cover it up, pretend it's not there,*
*and thus close ourselves off*
*from blessings that might come our way*
*if only we allowed ourselves to look.*
*An earlier English Charles, King Charles I,*
*just before he died on the scaffold in 1649,*
*put it rather well:*
*"I go from a corruptible crown*
*to an incorruptible crown,*
*where no disturbance can have place."*

# THE UNMISTAKABLE FRAGRANCE OF HYACINTH

Elaine's good friend, Ceil, fought a ten-year battle with cancer, but finally a tumor severed her spinal cord and left her paraplegic and almost totally blind. Planning to visit her friend in the hospital, Elaine decided to bring her a hyacinth plant because with her eyesight gone she wanted to bring something very fragrant that Ceil could enjoy.

Arriving at the hospital, Elaine entered Ceil's room, and immediately the delightful smell of the hyacinth plant filled the air. "While I prayed the rosary aloud," Elaine said, "she deeply inhaled the sweetness of the hyacinth. Although her body had been consumed by that disease there was no odor from her body."

One week after Ceil's funeral, Elaine and her sister entered their parish church for Sunday Mass, and they were greeted by the unmistakable fragrance of the hyacinth plant. "We looked around the altar and church, but there were no hyacinths," Elaine recalled. "We both said, 'Ceil!' I believe it was my friend's way of letting me know that she was in heaven with the Lord."

## Reflection

### From One Room to Another

*Before his death from cancer in 1981,*
*the great American writer William Saroyan*
*phoned the Associated Press*
*and dictated a final statement.*
*He said:*
*"Everybody has got to die,*
*but I have always believed*
*an exception would be made*
*in my case.*
*Now what?"*

*How like us all.*
*We all believe,*
*someplace deep inside,*
*that an exception will be made*
*in our case.*
*And in a way,*
*we're right.*
*It's just that the exception doesn't happen*
*here and now,*
*in a way other people can witness*
*and marvel at.*
*It happens on the other side*
*of an experience,*
*a transformation, we believe,*
*that we would just as soon avoid,*
*thank you very much.*
*Comic and filmmaker Woody Allen*
*put it succinctly years ago.*
*He said:*
*"I'm not afraid of dying,*
*I just don't want to be there*
*when it happens."*
*In spite of all the hints,*
*in spite of the occasional sign, even*
*—the aroma of hyacinths, for example,*
*where there are no hyacinths*
*—that death is not the end*
*but a new beginning,*
*we are naturally nervous*
*about dying.*
*It's okay to be nervous about death,*
*and it's probably unavoidable.*
*But we can still trust the whispers*
*of our heart.*
*As that famous author, Anonymous, wrote:*

*"The universe
is God's house.
In His house
are many rooms.
Death pushes aside
the door
that we may pass
from one room to another."*

# ELAINE'S SON RETURNS AFTER 9/11/01

In her book *Middletown, America* (Random House, 2003) author Gail Sheehy recounts the experience of Elaine and her son Swede who had a lifelong love for gardening and landscaping. Elaine's son was a recent graduate of Cornell University in business administration, and he and Elaine were going to be business partners. That morning, Elaine heard her son start his car to leave for his job in the World Trade Center. She thought of running down to give him a goodbye kiss, but instead she said a prayer asking the angel Raphael to "go with him."

Gail Sheehy wrote that "Swede's body was found, intact, several days after the tower in which he worked disintegrated. Thus Elaine was one of the few family members who knew, and knew early. She knew the literal truth—that her son would no longer live with her in this world—but where was he in the imponderable between earth and heaven?"

Elaine hoped for a sign. Six days after the tragedy, on a Monday, Elaine had a vision. In that remarkable place between sleeping and waking she saw the angel Raphael. The angel stood just behind Swede, looking at him with great tenderness. Elaine saw Swede standing by the side of a stream with white chrysanthemums on its banks. He smiled at his mother, and his yellow Lab was beside him—the dog he had loved who had died a few months earlier.

"Now that she reflected on it," Sheehy commented, "she understood that Swede's dog had gone ahead, as dogs do. The angel had lifted Swede out of the tower and spared him suffering and led him and his Lab to 'pass over' into the garden of all gardens."

Later that Monday, Elaine took a walk through some woods where she knew that Swede had recently found wild chrysanthemums. To nourish their roots, Swede had snipped off the buds and left them for mulch. Elaine was startled and amazed to see that the buds Swede had clipped off, completely unattached from their stems, lay on the ground in full bloom. It seemed to Elaine a message from Swede speaking through the flowers, a message of reassurance that there was nothing to be worried about.

Elaine decided to form a group with two other women who lost sons in the disaster of September 11, 2001. They would help the widows and mothers who lost husbands and sons to recover through spiritual support and guidance.

# THERE HE STOOD
# IN A RED FLANNEL SHIRT

One morning while folding freshly washed and dried laundry, Patricia felt someone's presence behind her. She turned around, and there stood her father, who had died a few years before. "He was wearing a red flannel shirt," Patricia said. "I didn't see his face, but I knew it was him, and I felt happy. I think he was letting me know that he was watching over me and that he loved me."

Patricia wasn't frightened at all by this experience. Later, telling her husband about what happened, she smiled happily. "I felt comforted by my father's visit. I think he visited me because I am far away from my brothers and sisters, and we are a very close family."

About six months later, Patricia's father showed up again. Patricia woke up one morning, her husband still asleep beside her, and there was her father sitting at the end of her bed, smiling. This time he wore a white short-sleeved shirt, and he stayed a little longer than before. No words were spoken by either Patricia or her father, but she believes that her dad was simply letting her know that he is still with her and taking care of her.

"I hope his visits do not stop," Patricia said.

# Reflection

## Time and Eternity

*Relationships with those we love*
*in this life*
*do not end.*
*Those we love*
*in time and space*
*continue to love us*
*after they make the transition*
*to that better life*
*we call "eternal."*
*Of course,*
*time and eternity are related.*
*As eighteenth-century English poet,*
*William Blake, wrote:*
*"To see a world in a grain of sand*
*And a heaven in a wild flower,*
*Hold infinity in the palm of your hand*
*And eternity in an hour."*
*The veil between time and eternity*
*is thin, indeed.*

# SURROUNDED BY LIGHT

Anne lay in bed, quiet but not asleep and definitely not dreaming. All of a sudden, she saw "a halo of shimmery, soft pink light," and in it was the face of her grandmother who had died six or seven years before.

"I was so startled," Anne said, "and I gasped when my grandmother said, 'I am so happy here.' She was so beautiful. This really strengthened my faith in God and his unending love."

Some time later, Anne said, she had an experience of God's love so overwhelming "it's hard to put into words."

Anne has "an undiagnosed neurological problem" which causes her, at times, to have excruciating muscle spasms. Only steroids and Valium (the commercial trade name for the tranquilizing drug diazepam) would relieve the pain and help the muscles relax.

On this occasion, Anne had been having painful muscle spasms for a few days, and this time the steroids and Valium gave her no relief. Anne went to a hospital where she was given a seventy-five milligram dose of Demerol (commercial trade name for synthetic morphine). "I felt strange almost immediately," Anne recalled, "and I told the medical people to come back and check on me soon."

In the next few minutes, Anne went from breathing just three times a minute to respiratory arrest, and she was put on a respirator to help her breathe. "As I lost consciousness, I remember feeling this wonderful feeling of peace, love, and security. I felt as if God's arms were wrapped around me, and he was loving me so much. I know it wasn't the drugs doing this because I had Demerol once or twice before, and I *never* felt like this."

Anne felt like God was holding her and loving her; she felt as a small child would feel who is hurt or scared and runs to his or her parents' arms for comfort. "The feeling was ten times more wonderful. I have *never* felt love like this!"

After this experience, Anne said, she is not afraid of death. She looks forward to God's love and being with him someday. Since this experience, Anne said, she knows that she was meant to stay on this earth a while and spread God's love. "He is now to me like a best friend I can talk to about my most personal needs and desires."

Anne belongs to a Bible study group, and she became a Big Sister in the Big Brothers/Big Sisters program. "I spend time with a child who is underprivileged. I feel that the laughter and joy and time I share with her is sharing God's love. Life is so fulfilling now, and I wish everyone could feel it as I do."

# Reflection

**Our Image of God**

*Sometimes we have the strangest ideas about God.*
*Many people think of God as*
*a great cosmic policeman,*
*or a hanging judge,*
*or some other forbidding or terrifying concept.*
*Tommy Bolt*
*was a famous golfer*
*in the early decades of the twentieth century.*
*He was also known*
*for his terrible temper.*
*One day, after sending six straight putts*
*right along the edge of the cup,*
*never in the cup,*
*Tommy Bolt shook his fist*
*at the heavens*
*and said,*
*"Why don't You come on down*
*and fight like a man!"*
*At that moment,*
*at least,*
*the great golfer's image of God*
*was of an eternal*
*Trickster,*
*a God who played mean tricks*

*on Tommy Bolt,*
*by keeping his putts*
*from rolling into the cup.*
*Not much of a God,*
*But are we so unlike Tommy Bolt?*
*Do we sometimes blame God*
*for the things that go wrong in everyday life?*
*What is the image of God*
*you work with daily?*
*One of the common messages*
*people bring back*
*from "near-death experiences"*
*is a message of feeling completely*
*loved and accepted.*
*Why should we be surprised by this?*
*Is this not the message of saints and prophets*
*all down the line?*
*God is love.*

# A VISIT FROM BROTHER BEN

Brother Thomas, a member of the Society of Mary ("Marianists"), a Roman Catholic religious community, remembers Brother Bernard—he was called "Ben"—fondly. Brother Thomas was assigned to teach at a Catholic high school in Baltimore, Maryland, and he found Brother Ben already on the faculty there.

One of Brother Ben's interests was flying, and he organized a small group of students into an aviation club at the high school. The school had a day off on a Monday, so Ben and three aviation club students decided to take advantage of the three-day weekend. They flew to Dayton, Ohio, to visit Wright Patterson Air Force Base. Dayton was also Ben's hometown.

"I met Ben as he was heading off for the airport," Thomas said. "I wished him and his student companions a good flight."

The weekend passed, and when Ben and the students did not return in time for classes the following Tuesday, no one thought much about it. Weather conditions could easily delay a return flight. But when two more days went by with no word from Brother Ben or the students, people began to worry. "I thought the principal must have heard from him by now," Brother Thomas said. "But by Thursday I learned that no one had heard anything."

Shortly after lunch on Friday, Thomas received word that Ben and his three students had been delayed by bad weather and had been unable to leave until Tuesday evening. Early Wednesday morning, they had crashed on South Mountain in western Maryland. "Workers had spotted the wreck. The state police had been called in. Tragedy struck. No one was spared."

During that terrible weekend, Thomas called a fellow Brother studying at Georgetown University to tell him the news, and the other Brother made the trip to Baltimore to visit Thomas. "As we talked that Friday night," Brother Thomas said, "I felt that I could tell him about my dream."

Thomas had gone to bed early Wednesday evening—11:45 P.M. was early for him, even if the religious community did begin its day at 5:30 A.M. He fell fast asleep and had a most remarkable dream. Thomas was involved in some activity and became aware that someone was watching him, and to impress the unseen visitor whose presence he felt, he renewed his efforts at what he was doing. "All of a sudden," Thomas said, "I literally felt negative energies leave my body. These were replaced with a full sense of physical well-being and a deep peace. From head to toe I was overcome with an intense delight."

As this was happening, Thomas became aware of Ben's presence, even though he did not see his face. "He was watching me. He himself was totally, completely happy."

Brother Thomas was so startled that he woke up. He sat on the side of his bed, the intense positive physical sensations still with him. He checked his clock to see what time it was. 1:26 A.M. Then Thomas easily went back to sleep. "I let the dream fade," he said, "until my friend from Georgetown arrived the night we

learned of Ben's death and the deaths of his three student companions."

Later, Thomas was given Ben's death certificate. He was to
become director of the Marianist community at the high school in
Baltimore, so his superiors wanted him to be aware of all that had
happened. When Brother Ben's plane crashed the wrist watches
worn by those in the plane had stopped, so they knew that the
crash had happened at 1:26 A.M., Wednesday. "That was the very
day and time I awoke from my night vision," Brother Thomas
said.

There is more to Thomas's story, however. Some months later,
he happened to be in Dayton, Ohio, and he went to visit Ben's
parents there. "I asked if I could keep a medallion of Saint Bernard that Ben had kept on his desk. They agreed to my request."

Wanting to be with Ben's parents in their grief, Thomas told
them about his dream and about how it had happened at the exact
time when their son was killed. "They were glad I told them about
my dream," Thomas said, "but they weren't at all surprised."

Brother Ben's parents had heard two other accounts of dreams
that took place the same time as the crash. One woman reported
her dream from Baltimore, and a cousin reported a dream from
Japan. "They both had ominous dreams of the disaster," Thomas
said; "I took mine as the single consolation. In large measure the
power of that dream stayed with me through the weekend of the
wake and funeral, a weekend no one who was there will ever forget."

# Reflection

## A Bigger God

*We are startled,*
*surprised,*
*perhaps perplexed,*
*maybe delighted*
*by stories such as this one.*

*But our feelings of surprise*
*reflect our lack of belief*
*in the reality of another life,*
*a better life,*
*beyond this one.*
*If we really believed in eternal life,*
*would such stories surprise us so much?*
*Arthur Rubenstein,*
*the great twentieth-century pianist,*
*was in the middle of an interview*
*on a radio program.*
*"Mr. Rubenstein,"*
*the interviewer said,*
*"Do you believe in God?"*
*"No," Rubenstein replied.*
*"You see, what I believe in*
*is something much greater."*
*Because "God" tends to be*
*such a limited idea*
*for many of us,*
*perhaps we could benefit*
*if we worked at trying to believe in*
*"something much greater."*
*This will help us*
*to expand our idea of reality*
*and help us to welcome*
*remarkable experiences*
*that our usual skepticism*
*might not be able to accept.*
*When we make room for*
*other sources of joy*
*we become deeper, wiser people*
*—the kind the world needs more of.*

# FILLED WITH GREAT PEACE

What is more difficult, to have a terminal illness oneself or be required to stand by while one's spouse suffers such an illness? In Pauline's case, when her husband, Tommy, was a victim of a long-term illness she received support in an unexpected way.

"It was very sad for me to see my husband lose interest in our business and to watch him decline in health," Pauline said. Then one day, Pauline was taking a nap. Suddenly, she awoke and there, beside her bed, was her husband's sister kneeling in prayer. She had been a nun and had died a few years before.

"Her face was hazy," Pauline recalled, "but I definitely knew it was her. In a few seconds, she faded away. I was filled with such peace by this visit. I felt strengthened to cope with my husband's illness."

A similar experienced happened for Pauline years later, after her husband had died. She remembers the exact date, December 9, because it was the day after a Catholic holy day, the Feast of the Immaculate Conception of Mary. It was approximately 3 A.M., and Pauline was asleep in her bed.

"All of a sudden," Pauline said, "I awoke and saw my deceased husband beside my bed. His face was hazy, but it was definitely him. It was a very peaceful experience to see Tommy again, and in a few seconds he faded away."

Remarkably, Tommy's appearance to Pauline happened on the anniversary of his death and the birthday of Pauline and her daughter which "made it so much easier to bear."

## Reflection

### Transcending Time and Space

*In a good marriage*
*you will find loving human intimacy*
*at its most complete.*

*This does not mean no conflict,*
*nor does it mean no hard times.*
*It certainly does not mean constant bliss.*
*It means, rather,*
*a union of hearts*
*that is stronger,*
*and more resilient*
*than any other form of human relationship.*
*Such a marriage*
*has such a deeply shared*
*kindness, compassion, and forgiveness,*
*and so much resilience*
*that the relationship between husband and wife*
*actually transcends time and space.*
*Joseph Hodges Choate,*
*the late nineteenth- and early twentieth-century lawyer*
*and diplomat,*
*was asked at a formal dinner*
*who he would like to be*
*if he were not himself.*
*He thought quickly through a list*
*of world celebrities,*
*and then,*
*catching his wife's eye, said,*
*"If I could not be myself,*
*I would like to be Mrs. Choate's*
*second husband."*
*In a marriage rooted in unselfishness,*
*passion,*
*acceptance and generosity,*
*it does not seem at all surprising*
*that a deceased partner*
*may "return"*
*in one form or another.*
*Love is that powerful.*

# A PRESENCE IN A DARKENED ROOM

The death of one's child is a particularly painful experience. In Roxie's case, she received comfort she could never have predicted.

Two weeks after the death of her twenty-one-year-old son, Mike, Roxie was lying in bed late at night, her whole being ravaged by soul-wrenching grief. "I suddenly felt a presence in the darkened room," she said. "I opened my eyes and Mike was standing before me with his arms outstretched to me. On his face was an expression of unbelief at the overwhelming sorrow I was feeling."

Then, Mike spoke. "Mother," he said softly, "it's okay, I'm all right, don't cry for me."

Roxie felt comforted instantly and knew "without a doubt" that she and Mike would be together again "in another time and another place with our Lord and Savior Jesus Christ."

## Reflection

### Love Takes a Chance

*Grief at the death of a child
can be profound.
After all, we think,
it isn't right
that parents
should outlive their child.
Thales was a Greek philosopher
who lived from about 640 to 546 B.C.E.
Once Thales entertained
the great Athenian lawgiver, Solon.
Solon teased Thales, asking him
why he did not marry
and have children.*

*Thales made no reply.*
*Soon after this,*
*a stranger came to Thales' house.*
*Thales took him aside*
*for a few words*
*before introducing him to Solon.*
*Approaching the great philosopher,*
*the stranger informed Solon*
*that he came from Athens.*
*Solon eagerly asked for any news*
*of his home city.*
*"No news," said the stranger,*
*"apart from the funeral of a great man's son."*
*"Who's son was this?" Solon inquired.*
*"I cannot remember the name," replied the stranger,*
*"but the father is a man of great honor,*
*who is currently traveling abroad."*
*His feelings of foreboding growing all the while,*
*Solon burst out,*
*"Was it the son of Solon?"*
*"Yes, that was the name," said the stranger.*
*When Solon began to weep,*
*and express extreme grief,*
*Thales took him by the hand*
*and said gently,*
*"These things that can strike down*
*even a man as resolute as Solon*
*with uncontrollable grief*
*are the things that prevent me from marrying*
*and raising a family.*
*But take courage,*
*not a word of the man's story is true."*
*The mistake Thales made,*
*of course,*
*was to deprive himself of marriage*
*and children*

*based on the possibility*
*that they might die*
*and cause him great sadness.*
*If we followed his example,*
*we would never know love,*
*friendship,*
*or any form of human intimacy.*
*To follow the example of Thales*
*is to be a coward,*
*and to reject the belief*
*—sometimes borne out by amazing experiences*
*—that our loved ones who die*
*are still with us,*
*and some eternal day we will be with them.*

# COMFORT FROM A
# DECEASED HUSBAND

Sometimes, after the death of a spouse, the tendency is for the surviving spouse to continue in the daily patterns established before the other partner passed away. This was the case with Grace. Some two months after the death of her husband, she was reclining on the couch in her living room, rather absentmindedly watching television, just as she and her husband used to do each evening. "I had no thought in mind," Grace said, "except how lonely I was."

Soon—and Grace doesn't know if she fell asleep or not—she felt herself "being lifted bodily in midair with the most beautiful feeling I have ever felt in my life. A tremendous peace came over me. I don't think there is any word in the dictionary to describe this kind of peace."

While still in midair, Grace looked over to where her husband usually sat in his club chair, and there he was watching her. "With that, I came back to reality. I just felt good and sort of put it out of my mind."

About two weeks later the same thing happened again, and again Grace dismissed the whole experience from her mind.

A few weeks later, Grace had gone to bed for the night. She still slept on the same side of the bed as when her husband was alive. After a few hours of sleep, she felt someone in bed with her. "I turned my head and there was my husband looking at me. I asked him why he didn't have his arm around me for this is how we fell asleep every night. He looked at me and walked out of the room. I woke up and finally realized that my husband was coming to visit me and tell me he was watching over me."

Grace's husband did not visit her again, but, she says, "I know he is there for me. For years I have wanted to shout it over the rooftops because of the unnatural peace that came over me with these three visits."

# Reflection

### Loving Relationships Go On

*So many of the stories*
*about "encounters" of various kinds*
*with deceased loved ones*
*are, at rock bottom,*
*stories about the transcendence of love.*
*A loving relationship does not end*
*when the mortal life of one person*
*comes to its conclusion.*
*So many of the stories*
*about "encounters" with deceased loved ones*
*are stories about the continuation of love.*
*They are stories*
*about how weak,*
*in this world,*
*are faith, hope, and love.*
*They are stories*
*about how triumphant*

*in the next world*
*is life itself.*
*Those who "pass over"*
*into the life we call "eternal"*
*have no fear,*
*they are not anxious or worried.*
*All they do is love,*
*and when they "return,"*
*invariably,*
*their message to us is one of*
*unconditional love.*
*In other words,*
*they remind us of what*
*we already know,*
*that "love is from God" and*
*"everyone who loves*
*is born of God*
*and knows God" (1 John 4:7).*
*It's as simple,*
*and profound,*
*as that.*
*Our lives are so conditioned*
*by anxiety and fear.*
*Yet there is, in the end,*
*no need for fear,*
*no need for fear,*
*no need for fear.*
*The opposite of fear*
*is not security.*
*The opposite of fear*
*is trust,*
*and only the person who loves*
*can trust completely.*
*"Love seeks one thing only,"*
*said Thomas Merton:*

*"the good of the one loved.*
*It leaves all the other secondary effects*
*to take care of themselves.*
*Love, therefore,*
*is its own reward."*

# "I HEARD HIS VOICE"

There seems to be no pattern to the experience of a loved one after his or her death. Sometimes it happens, sometimes it doesn't. There is also no pattern as to where and when.

Kathleen's father died following several years of illness. After her father's death, Kathleen said, she "was in such agony about the welfare of his soul that I prayed and prayed for him as I'd never prayed in my life." Kathleen also "fell into the deepest despair I'd ever experienced and came perilously close to losing my faith, because I was certain I'd never again, in any fashion, see or know my father again."

The August after her father's death, Kathleen was home alone, gardening, her husband and son being out of town. "Of course, I was praying and grieving for my father," she said. "Suddenly, I heard his voice speaking to me. His voice had been remarkably deep and resonant for a man as ill and weak as he had become. In fact, that was the only part of his physical makeup that had not deteriorated greatly. His voice was instantly recognizable, and at the moment I recognized his voice I also realized it had not come through my ears but directly to whatever part of the brain receives sounds. There were only six words, lasting perhaps ten seconds: 'Little daughter, I'm proud of you.'"

Kathleen's father belonged to a generation of men who often found it difficult to say, "I love you," which lends authenticity to the words she heard. Her father simply would not have said, "I love you." "Little daughter, I'm proud of you," sounded exactly like him.

After this astounding experience, Kathleen put down her gardening tools, went into the house, sat down and asked herself, "Did I really hear that?" She had never wanted or expected such an experience. She had never believed such a thing could happen to her. "It was quite literally inconceivable," she said. "But after a period of both shock and reflection, I was convinced that it had happened—I *did* hear my father's voice."

Reflecting on her remarkable experience, Kathleen concluded: "This totally unsolicited and unexpected experience meant not only that my father's soul had survived physical death, but that as a result of this knowledge I could cherish my faith again."

A few months later, Kathleen's husband died, yet "despite a terrible and depressing sense of loss, I have not experienced the despair or weakening of faith I had known following my father's death. I believe I received a once-in-a-lifetime gift from my father so that I could live on with faith despite the worst loss I could imagine, that of my wonderful husband, Jack.

Kathleen happened to find a prayer by the late Hubert Van Zeller, called "A Prayer for Someone Lately Dead," in an old book titled *Come Lord*. The prayer begins, "The nearer a soul comes to thee, Lord, the happier it must become. And the happier it is the more it must want to share its happiness with others. May this soul for whom I pray come quickly to thy presence, and finding there it's longed-for peace, may it find a means of communicating something of its joy to us."

# Reflection

### A Word of Love

*We are loved,*
*and we are meant to have joy.*
*This is it,*
*this is all we need to know,*
*yet we have such a difficult time*
*remembering this truth.*

*So often we find ourselves*
*weighed down*
*by the burdens of the world.*
*We forget that we are loved*
*with an infinite, unconditional*
*love.*
*We become dissatisfied,*
*frustrated,*
*anxious*
*and fearful.*
*And why?*
*Sometimes we have real, justifiable*
*worries.*
*Someone we love is terribly sick,*
*or financial insecurity weighs us down,*
*or we become depressed*
*for no apparent reason.*
*More of the time, however,*
*we are dissatisfied*
*because the feeling grows in us*
*like a cancer,*
*a dark unhappiness*
*that we believe will go away*
*if only we can have something we do not have.*
*If we can have new furniture,*
*new appliances,*
*a new car,*
*a new television set,*
*a new wardrobe...*
*The mass media advertising industry*
*convinces us*
*that we need, must have, cannot live without*
*something that looks very attractive, indeed,*
*in television commercials*
*and slick, full-color magazine ads.*
*But that's not it,*

*that is a despicable deception.*
*We need a few basics,*
*a few comforts,*
*even a few extras.*
*But in the end all of our craving,*
*all of our emptiness,*
*and all of our longing,*
*add up to one desire:*
*the desire for God*
*who is love.*
*Saint Augustine of Hippo,*
*some fifteen centuries ago,*
*said it better than anyone before or since.*
*Augustine prayed to the God he knew as Love:*
*"...you have made us for yourself,*
*and our heart is restless*
*until it rests in you."*
*We long to hear this word.*
*As children, we long to hear it from our parents.*
*As adults, we still long to hear it from our parents.*
*And to hear this word of love*
*from a deceased father or mother*
*is an extraordinary gift,*
*one that is bound to touch the heart.*
*Of course, we long, above all,*
*to hear this word of love*
*from our Creator.*
*It's not difficult to hear.*
*All we need do is sit quietly*
*and listen to our own heart*
*Fifteen minutes of quiet listening,*
*perhaps some quiet asking to hear this word,*
*and we are sure to hear it*
*whenever we need to hear it.*

# AN ARM ACROSS MY SHOULDERS

Frances's husband, Bill, died after nearly forty years of marriage. A few weeks later, she was not only sorrowful at having lost him but she felt disappointed because she wasn't dreaming about him at night, something she "wanted desperately."

Later, Frances read someplace that if you pray for a loved one to show you his or her presence, that will happen. "That's exactly what I did that night," Frances said. "Early the next morning, I dreamed that I felt the weight of someone's arm across my shoulders, but I was not afraid. I said, 'Is that you, Bill?' and he said, 'Yes.'"

In her dream, Frances opened her eyes and saw her husband lying next to her, and she kissed his cheek. "I said, 'I miss you very much,' and all he said was, 'I know.' I woke up right after that, but it was as if I could still feel the weight of his arm on my back. I really felt that Bill had been there and that he knew the pain I was suffering. It also made me feel somewhat tranquil. My loneliness seemed a little more bearable."

Frances told her cousin, whose husband died a month before Bill. "She said that her husband came to her one night surrounded by light. She was in bed but she swears she was awake. Her husband didn't say anything, but he stood at the foot of her bed and smiled at her. She took this as a sign that things would turn out all right for her, and it left her with a peaceful feeling."

## Reflection

### Love Is Ultimately Meaningful

*It's wonderful*
*to experience the presence*
*of a loved one now gone,*
*now living a new and better life.*
*But those of us who do not have such experiences*
*can learn from those who do.*

*Werner von Braun,*
*the famous German-American space technology pioneer,*
*said:*
*"Everything science has taught me*
*—and continues to teach me*
*—strengthens my belief in the continuity*
*of our spiritual existence*
*after death."*
*In other words,*
*there is more than one way*
*to gain the blessed assurance*
*that life has meaning here and now,*
*and there is more than one way*
*to gain the blessed assurance*
*that on the other side of natural death*
*we will find overwhelming love*
*and unconditional acceptance.*
*This knowledge may be gained*
*from the study of science,*
*as happened for Werner von Braun.*
*We may find it by reflecting on the love*
*we have for others,*
*and the love they have for us.*
*Does it seem likely*
*that love is ultimately meaningless?*
*The absurdity of this proposition*
*has gargantuan proportions.*
*We may gain this same assurance*
*by a simple observation of nature, too.*
*As did William Jennings Bryan,*
*who said:*
*"If the Father deigns to touch with divine power*
*the cold and pulseless heart of the buried acorn*
*and to make it burst forth*
*from its prison walls,*
*will He leave neglected*

*in the earth*
*the soul of man*
*made in the image of his Creator?"*
*Not likely.*

# THE LAST AND BEST GIFT

For many years, Joanne took the reality of an afterlife "on faith." Still, it was the belief she struggled with the most...until something happened.

Joanne's maternal grandmother suffered from Parkinson's disease for thirty years, for all of Joanne's life. "She had a wrinkled, diseased face and hands that shook," Joanne said. "She used to joke about it. We had been quite close for a while, but I moved four hundred miles away in order to attend graduate school."

After she moved, Joanne did not keep in close contact with her grandmother. When her grandmother died, Joanne wondered if her grandmother had been upset with her for not being better about staying in touch.

About one year after her death, Joanne said, "she came to me in a dream. Her face was radiant and healed of all disease and pain. She was beautiful. I saw her face in my dream, talking to me. I never remembered her words, but her mere presence filled me with peace. I have been filled with assurance that heaven is a reality. It was Grandma's final and best gift to me."

## Reflection

**Sacred Dreams**

*Dreams are mysterious,*
*no matter how you look at them.*
*Yet it would be foolish to dismiss dreams*
*as nothing but the meanderings of the psyche*

*while we are asleep.*
*Saint Thomas Aquinas said*
*that dreams can come from God.*
*In the Bible, astonishing messages come from God*
*in dreams.*
*In the Book of Genesis (37:5-7),*
*Joseph has a corker of a dream,*
*and when he tells it to his brothers,*
*they hate him even more*
*than they did before.*
*"He said to them, 'Listen to this dream that I dreamed.*
*There we were,*
*binding sheaves in the field.*
*Suddenly my sheaf rose and stood upright;*
*then your sheaves gathered around it,*
*and bowed down to my sheaf.'"*
*God speaks to Jacob and many others*
*in dreams.*
*Angels appear in dreams*
*with messages from God.*
*Joseph, the husband of Mary,*
*receives instructions in dreams*
*to do things that require*
*much trouble and inconvenience.*
*Packing up for a long trek*
*to Bethlehem, for example.*
*Packing up for an even longer trek*
*to Egypt, for example.*
*Psychologists poke around in dreams,*
*trying to interpret them,*
*which is fine.*
*But let us not overlook*
*a more poetic perspective.*
*Let us not overlook the possibility*
*of a sacred dimension.*

*Especially in situations*
*where people dream of a deceased loved one,*
*let us not overlook the fact*
*that we are mysterious beings,*
*and who is to say that spirit and body*
*may not cooperate in the service*
*of that which is holy*
*in us.*

# KEEPING IN TOUCH

Frances and her husband were happily married for seventeen years. Then he died of a congenital kidney disease. Frances was left with three children, a boy age fifteen and two girls, eight and ten.

"I went through a very severe spell of depression from the agony of loss," Frances said.

After several weeks of troubled sleep and listless days, one morning Frances woke to the sound of her children squabbling in the kitchen as they got ready to leave for school. She had a nightmare in which she was running after her husband, calling, "Wait, wait!" but he kept running away from her. Frances felt so bad that she dreaded getting up. "I just wanted to die," she said. "That's how bad I felt."

Suddenly, through the bedroom door came her husband. He was dressed as he had been when she first met him, his wide-brim hat pushed back on his head at a jaunty angle. "He had a big smile on his face," Frances said, "and it was like a wind was blowing on him. He came over to the bed and knelt down, and put his arms around me. He said, 'You must not pine, you must not feel bad anymore. I'm right beside you. Remember, I am here with you always. You mustn't cry, you will be happy.' Then it was like he went down through the floor.

"I got up from bed, and all the bad feelings were gone. I was afraid that I would lose the glory of it within the month, so I wrote a poem about my experience that tells it all. I'm so glad I did. There is something very precious and special about this. Except for my own children I have hugged it to myself these many years."

# Reflection

### Death Isn't the Final Word

*Relationships*
*are so basic to who we are,*
*so much a part of our identity,*
*that when a person we love dearly*
*dies,*
*we often feel as if*
*a part of us*
*is dead, too.*
*How can we go on*
*without the one*
*we loved so much?*
*Depression following the death*
*of a dearly beloved person*
*is not uncommon*
*and quite understandable.*
*When we feel that a part of our very self*
*has been torn away from us,*
*we are likely to lose much*
*of our own will to live.*
*We are likely to wonder*
*why we should go on*
*making the effort.*
*Why get out of bed*
*in the morning?*
*The message of faith,*
*however,*
*is the same message*
*bereaved persons sometimes receive*

*from a deceased loved one.*
*Death is real,*
*to be sure,*
*but death is not the ultimate end*
*either of the person*
*or of our relationship*
*with the one who died.*
*Everything is transformed*
*mysteriously.*
*"There is nothing innocent or good,"*
*Charles Dickens said,*
*"that dies and is forgotten:*
*let us hold to that faith*
*or none."*

## "SIGNALS" FROM HEAVEN

Encounters with deceased loved ones aren't always apparitions or a matter of hearing a loved one's voice or feeling his or her presence. In *Loved Beyond Life: The Healing Power of After-Death Communications* (HarperCollins, 1997) Joel Martin and Patricia Romanowski share accounts from people whose deceased loved ones sent clear "signals" from heaven to reassure and comfort those they left behind.

A woman said that sometimes she feels sad and wishes that her brother was still alive to give her a hug. No matter when this happens, or where she is, she hears her brother's favorite song coming from a radio.

A man whose wife died reported that on several occasions when he was at home, around breakfast time, he has smelled cinnamon rolls being heated in the microwave. "That was my wife's favorite breakfast treat. I knew it was her, because I haven't had those rolls in the house since she died. I know it's her."

Not long after her mother died, a woman bought an angel-wing begonia because, she said, something about the plant with its large, ruffled, gray-tinged leaves and rich, rose-colored blossoms reminded her of her mother. The plant bloomed the first year she had it, then never again after that. Fifteen years later, this women came home from her doctor's office having learned that she had miscarried a baby. "I was thinking about how much I still missed my mother. Then I noticed that the plant was in bloom."

## Reflection

### "Signals" Can Be Clear

*So often, the trouble with our scientific inclinations
is that they alienate us from our deeper
ways of knowing.
Sure, we can kid ourselves sometimes.
But perceptions and intuitions
can be just as trustworthy as
the most rigorous scientific data.
Sometimes, more so.
When a deceased relative or friend
sends a "signal" from heaven
we can take it at face value.
Why not?*

# BRILLIANT LIGHT
# FLOODED AROUND HIM

"Our son Kevin, age twenty-seven when he died, was a remarkable boy," George said. "According to a woman who worked with him...he 'was never too busy to help anyone in need.' She told us this at Kevin's...funeral when we and his wife of five years released him back to God."

One winter evening, at about 8 P.M., Kevin stopped his car to help a stranger get his vehicle out of a snowdrift. The wind was blowing, and it was very cold. Suddenly, another car came along, and as Kevin's wife watched in horror as the car slid on the icy road and hit Kevin. "He died in her arms as she sat on the street in the snow holding him."

A year later, Kevin's younger brother, Christopher, who is a carpenter, slipped on a roof where he was doing some repair work. "He tore loose a muscle in his knee so badly," George explained, "that it necessitated an operation the next day."

For a young carpenter in business for himself, with a wife and two young children, the outlook was bleak, indeed. "Christopher had always been close to Kevin," George said. "They had the same birthday, April 4, and each year their common birthday seemed to bring them closer together. They were born only three years apart." Now, as Christopher lay alone in a hospital bed, he felt Kevin's absence acutely. But then, Chris said, everything changed. "He cried," George recalled, "as he told his mother and me that suddenly brilliant light seemed to flood around him, and he had a deep feeling of great joy and happiness. He felt that Kevin was very near, 'in the next room,' he said, 'but I couldn't open the door, and all was so beautiful and glorious that I knew Kevin was there. I knew he was in heaven and helping me. It was wonderful. I could sense his presence and I was so thrilled by it all.'"

Chris soon recovered from his operation and returned to work, and he has enjoyed good health ever since.

## Reflection

### Living on the Porch

*Most of the time,*
*we don't realize*
*how deeply we are shaped*
*by the modern scientific world view.*
*Science*
*limits itself*

to what the five senses can discover.
Unless we can see it,
hear it,
touch it,
taste it,
and/or smell it,
science refuses to believe it is real.
This is why we are so amazed
when we experience
—with our senses
—realities that science cannot explain.
Should comfort
and encouragement
come from the sphere of
eternity,
we tend to doubt our own senses.
Now and then, however,
the experience is so overwhelming
and so obviously real
that all we can do
is believe.
At times such as this,
in the words of Frederick W. Faber,
a nineteenth-century English writer,
"We cannot resist the conviction
that this world is
for us
only the porch of another
and more magnificent temple
of the Creator's majesty."

# HAPPINESS DISPELS THE GLOOM

George has another story about Kevin. A friend who is a former state commissioner of education, described a remarkable experience.

"After seven hours of intense surgery for prostate cancer," George said, "he lay on the hospital bed in the Intensive Care Unit. It was late afternoon, and he was hooked up to all sorts of monitors, and he was exhausted. At four o'clock the nurses' shift changed, and for a few moments he felt very alone, his spirits pretty low."

Prior to his friend's surgery, without going into detail, George had told him about Kevin and his brother, Chris's, experience. As their friend lay in his hospital bed, for some reason he thought about Kevin. "In his desolation," George said, "strangely, he began to pray to him."

All of a sudden everything changed. "The gloom became flooded with light and happiness; joy took over his heart, and he seemed to sense someone was near. All was different, though he could not explain it."

George immediately saw how similar their friend's experience had been to that of their son, Chris. "Like Chris, he has enjoyed good health ever since the experience."

## Reflection

**Living With Delight**

*We are delighted
with stories like this one,
stories of wonderful changes
apparently accomplished
by people who died.
We delight in the apparent fact
that someone who was good
during their earthly life*

*would go on doing good*
*after he or she*
*passed over the Great Divide.*
*It is good that we should be delighted.*
*But at the same time,*
*we should not be so*
*surprised.*
*Why should good people*
*and the good deeds they do*
*be limited to this world?*
*Why should they not continue?*
*An early twentieth-century writer,*
*Nathan Soderblom,*
*said:*
*"Saints are persons*
*who make it easier for others*
*to believe in God."*

# A HAND OF REASSURANCE

Mary has had several major surgeries, and always when she is recovering from the anesthesia she gets very ill, including constant vomiting, sometimes lasting as long as eight hours. Also, it takes Mary a long time to wake up, so she is only half conscious of what is going on. Her mother was always at Mary's side to help when she came out of the recovery room.

Two years after Mary's mother died, she had to have another surgery. As she lay in recovery, Mary remembers thinking about her mother and about the fact that she would not be with her to help out this time. "That night, I was so sick, struggling to help myself and missing her so much. I dozed off to sleep and during the night I felt a hand on my shoulder."

At first, Mary thought she was feeling the hand of a nurse waking her for some reason. "I opened my eyes, there was no one in the room, and the light was off. At once I felt the presence of my mother. I spoke to her and said, 'Mom, is it you?' I felt her love and a sense of comfort as if she was telling me, 'Yes, I am here.'

"This experience," Mary commented, "brought home to me what I believed, that love does not die and that our loved ones are always looking out for us. I will never forget the firm touch that woke me, and I know she was there!"

# Reflection

## Open to the Possibilities

*Why do such marvelous experiences
happen for some people
but not for others?
Actually,
they seem to happen to a great many more people
than is commonly believed.
At the same time,
encounters with deceased loved ones
clearly don't happen to everyone.
Perhaps some people would not benefit
from such an experience.
They might be frightened, perhaps,
and that would be the end of that.
But there's another perspective.
Perhaps more people
would have such experiences
if they were open to the possibility.
Perhaps we need to expect
to feel the love and encouragement
of deceased relatives or friends
before it will happen.
Or, perhaps it's best to cultivate
a holy indifference.*

## SMILES FROM MY MOM

Rebecca's mother had been dead for more than ten years. One August morning, she arose at about 6 A.M. to let her dogs outside. Once the dogs were out, Rebecca turned and walked through her living room toward another bedroom. As she approached the bedroom door and put her hand on the doorknob, out of the corner of her eye she saw a brilliant golden-white light.

"As I instantly swung around to face the light, there in all her beauty stood my precious mother. She was beautiful beyond words! Standing in this light—or rather, she *was* this light—she looked thirty-five to forty years of age, instead of sixty-seven, which she was when she passed on. Of course, I absorbed everything I saw at that moment, and it was totally captivating.

"There stood my mother not more than a few feet away, smiling broadly at me. I was so overjoyed I instinctively screamed, "MAMA!" practically leaping into her arms."

Rebecca and her mother "hugged and kissed and laughed, and hugged again and again." Then, as Rebecca was hugging her mother she noticed how "solid" she was. She said, "Mama, Mama...I can feel you! It's really you!" Saying that, Rebecca stepped back to look at her mother again...and she was gone.

"I knew she had manifested herself to me for that one special moment," Rebecca said. "It was indeed enough, for I will carry it with me until we meet again. And we *will* meet again, for LOVE lives forever, and we were very close."

Rebecca adds that experiences such as this one can give hope to those who cannot see deceased relatives and friends. "But I can hardly describe the personal joy and elation one feels through a reunion with a deceased loved one. It would be like trying to describe the scent of a rose to someone who had no sense of smell."

# Reflection

### A Pure Gift

*For those of us*
*who do not experience the presence*
*of a deceased relative or friend,*
*what does it mean*
*that such things happen to others*
*but not to us?*
*Perhaps we feel disappointed.*
*But it may be that such experiences*
*are like events we call miracles.*
*They seem to happen randomly,*
*but they happen to encourage everyone,*
*not just the person they happen to.*
*At the same time,*
*those who do have encounters*
*of one kind or another*
*with a deceased relative or friend,*
*have no room to brag.*
*Clearly, no one*
*deserves such an experience.*
*They are a pure gift,*
*given to the undeserving*
*for the benefit of all.*

# A HUSBAND SAYS "I LOVE YOU..."

"My beloved husband of thirty-two years passed away on March 25," said Barbara. His favorite hymn was a song by Michael Joncas, "On Eagle's Wings," and Barbara had this song played at her husband's funeral Mass.

As the couple's thirty-third wedding anniversary approached,

Barbara began to dread the day. "I wondered how on earth I would get through it," she said.

As she drove home from work the day before their anniversary, Barbara was crying and becoming more and more upset by the minute, wondering if she could have done more for him. Why hadn't I become aware of his illness sooner? "My mind was filled with 'what ifs' and 'if onlys,'" she said.

Through her tears, Barbara prayed that her husband would forgive her for any shortcomings. "The thought of getting through the next day had me in a state of near panic," she said.

For no particular reason, Barbara turned on her car radio, even though the last thing she wanted to do right then was listen to the radio. "Immediately," she recalled, "the most beautiful tenor voice began singing, 'On Eagle's Wings.' I pulled over to the curb and just listened. It is not a very popular hymn, and for it to come on the radio at all, let alone at that precise moment, was to me a miracle. It was like a message from my husband saying, 'I love you. Don't beat yourself up—there's nothing to forgive.'"

Barbara described the next day, she and her late husband's anniversary, as "serene and beautiful." Even though she misses her husband terribly, she said, "I have felt the most wonderful sense of peace ever since that day because I know for sure that love never dies.

"Even though my husband is gone from this life," Barbara concluded, "he gave me the best anniversary present he could ever have given me."

# Reflection

### The Ordinary Is Holy

*Comfort*
*and a renewal of our spirit*
*can come in the most ordinary ways.*
*It doesn't always happen*
*that people have spectacular experiences*

*—a deceased loved one appearing in person,*
*or amazing visions of various kinds.*
*Because the most ordinary event*
*can communicate the sacred to us,*
*sometimes the most overwhelming comfort*
*and joy can come in the most ordinary way.*
*Because the ordinary*
*is holy,*
*a song on a car radio*
*can have as much of an impact*
*as a deceased friend or relative*
*appearing in person*
*or in a dream.*

# THE BRIDGE OF SORROW

Mildred's husband had a dream in which her brother, Bill, guided him across a collapsing bridge. "Bill kept urging him on," Mildred said, "telling him, 'Don't worry, I'll get you across safely.'"

A few weeks later, Mildred's husband went into the hospital for surgery on his pancreas. "Though it was a delicate operation," Mildred said, "within months he had recovered nicely. I sensed the collapsing bridge represented my husband's body, and my brother was there for its repair."

One of Mildred's daughters saw Mildred's deceased brother, Harry, in a dream. "He put his hand on her shoulder and said, 'Don't let Mom know yet that I am here.'"

This daughter later had to be rushed to the hospital when she started to bleed heavily. "They discovered a tubular pregnancy and a cyst on her ovary," Mildred said. "Fortunately, they were able to operate, and she has recovered, I believe through the presence of my brother, Harry."

One night in a dream, Mildred was with a group of people when her brother, Lee, arrived. "I became frightened and said,

'What are you doing here? You're dead.' He left right away, and I awoke from the dream."

Not long after this, Mildred lost control of her right eyelid. After many tests, the doctors discovered that Mildred had two aneurysms in her head, one very large, the other smaller. "I know now," she said, "that though my siblings have entered eternal life, through the grace of God they were there for our protection and brought us all through safely."

When Mildred and her family moved into a new home, they became friends with Mae and Frank, their next-door neighbors, who were twenty years older than she and her husband. About ten years later, Frank became ill with cancer and died within a few months. Mae stayed on in their house for a few more years, then sold the house and moved in with her daughter.

Marge and Joe, who bought the house, had three children. "Marge would come over for coffee and conversation," Mildred recalled, "and our children played together."

One morning, Marge asked Mildred if she knew anyone who wore a brown striped suit and smoked cigars. The only person Mildred knew who fit that description was Mae's late husband, Frank, the previous occupant of Marge and Joe's house. Marge said that as she was watching TV, "a figure glided past her and a strong smell of cigar smoke permeated the air. This happened a second time, too."

Later, Mildred learned that Frank's wife, Mae, was ill. She died several months later. "I assume," Mildred said, "that Frank returned to the house which was his last home on earth."

One day, Mildred's youngest daughter was visiting Marge, as Marge often worked on crafts with Mildred's children or played games with them. The phone rang, and Mildred's daughter stood leaning against the frame of the kitchen door, bag of marbles in hand, waiting for Marge to finish her telephone conversation.

"My daughter felt a strange sensation from her feet to her knees," Mildred said, "and she was picked up, turned completely around, and set back down on the floor still standing but with one leg crossed over the other.

"Marge said, 'How did you do that? You were at least eighteen inches off the floor!'"

When Marge related the incident to Mildred, she asked if Frank had known her daughter. Mildred said that he had known her when she was just a baby. "He used to play 'Daddy's Little Girl' on his violin for her," Mildred said.

## Reflection

### Join the Cosmic Dance

*Playful spirits?*
*Why not?*
*Thomas Merton,*
*the widely influential Trappist monk and author,*
*wrote that God plays, so why not human spirits?*
*In a famous passage*
*in his 1961 classic,*
New Seeds of Contemplation,
*Merton wrote:*
*"What is serious to men*
*is often very trivial in the sight of God.*
*What in God might appear to us as 'play'*
*is perhaps what He Himself*
*takes most seriously.*
*At any rate,*
*the Lord plays and diverts Himself*
*in the garden of His creation,*
*and if we could let go*
*of our own obsession*
*with what we think is the meaning of it all,*
*we might be able to hear His call*
*and follow Him*
*in His mysterious,*
*cosmic dance."*

# "I SAW MY DECEASED MOTHER"

Edna had a successful gall bladder operation, and she looked forward to a speedy recovery. Instead, she found herself back in the hospital three days later with a blood clot in her lung. One night during her hospital stay she had a dream.

"I saw my deceased mother standing a few feet away from me," Edna recalled. "She was dressed in a long white robe and was accompanied by a small child also garbed in white. This may have been my cousin, Frances, who died at six years of age. Not one word was spoken, but I received the message, 'NOT YET.'"

During this dream, Edna said, she felt "the most blissful sense of peace and joy. It was sheer ecstasy. I have never experienced anything like it in this world. I do believe my mother brought a little bit of heaven with her."

## Reflection

**This Life Is a Gift**

*So often,*
*the result of an encounter*
*with a deceased relative or friend*
*is an ecstatic feeling of peace and joy.*
*What might we learn from this?*
*We might learn that death*
*is nothing to be afraid of.*
*We might learn that*
*the goodness and joy of this life*
*are but a hint of what awaits us*
*on the other side.*
*We might also learn*
*that no matter how difficult*
*or painful*
*this life may be at times,*

*there is no need to think*
*that this is the end.*
*There is always more.*
*At the same time,*
*people who have such experiences*
*never report receiving a message*
*to give up on this life because the next life*
*is so much better.*
*On the contrary,*
*this life is a gift to be lived*
*to the last drop,*
*all the joy*
*and all the anguish.*
*Somehow, it all has meaning*
*for this life*
*and for the next life, as well.*

# UNCLE FREDDIE COMES TO CALL

Nancy recalls that her mother's brother, Freddie, was "a loner." He would come around from time to time to say hello or get a few dollars from Nancy's mother, but when she didn't hear from him she didn't try to make contact.

"When the news came that Freddie died, my mother grieved out of loss, but mostly because she felt guilty," Nancy said. "My sisters and brothers and I worried about Mom's health because of this grief."

One afternoon, as Nancy's mother was washing clothes, she heard a knock at the door and went to answer it. "At her door," Nancy said, "was my Uncle Freddie. He looked at my mom and said, 'Fay, what are you doing to yourself? Stop. I can't rest.' And with this he disappeared."

Nancy's mother stopped grieving, and her health improved. "Was this my uncle," Nancy wondered, "or a messenger from God?

All I know is that God sent someone to help my mother because of his love for his children."

# Reflection

### The Focus Is Here

*Notice*
*that the focus of all the stories*
*in this book is not*
*the next world*
*but this one.*
*The sadness,*
*grief,*
*and pain of loss*
*suffered by people right here,*
*right now,*
*is relieved by a touch from*
*the eternal realm.*
*This may encourage fascination with*
*the next life.*
*But in these stories the concern of those already in*
*the next life*
*is this life.*
*Perhaps the lesson for us is*
*that it's fine to be surprised and delighted,*
*but we should attend most of the time*
*to more pressing concerns*
*here and now.*
*If we do this, the next life*
*—and our part in it—*
*will take care of itself.*
*Preparations will be made*
*for our arrival.*
*Certainly the next life does not preoccupy*
*those we might call "living saints"*

*—Mother Teresa of Calcutta—*
*for example*
*—who would seem to have*
*the most to look forward to.*
*Her focus is the needs of others*
*right here, right now.*
*We would do well to do likewise*
*in our own little corner of the world.*

# A LAUGHING AND
# SMILING BARBARA

Nancy's sister Barbara was dying of breast cancer at the age of forty-eight. Phyllis, another of Nancy's sisters, made the trip from her home in New Jersey to take her and Nancy's mother to visit Barbara in Long Island, New York. As it turned out, Barbara died at home during the night prior to her mother's planned visit.

"While waiting for my sister, Phyllis, to pick her up at her apartment in Brooklyn," Nancy said, "standing in her kitchen Mom saw Barbara laughing and smiling—very happy. Then Barbara disappeared. I believe that God sent Barbara to Mom to ease the pain of her daughter's death and to show her that Barbara was very happy to be with Jesus...."

## Reflection

**The Only Way to Live**

*The ultimate fear,*
*philosophers and psychologists tell us,*
*is the fear of death.*
*We can trace all our other fears,*
*small and large,*
*to our fear of death.*

*On the level of the unconscious,*
*we adopt all kinds of tactics*
*to avoid thinking of death.*
*We do not want to think about our own*
*mortality.*
*"Why be morbid?"*
*we may ask.*
*But there is nothing necessarily morbid*
*about pondering the reality of death.*
*No need to be preoccupied with it,*
*of course.*
*But from time to time,*
*it's healthy to consider our own mortality.*
*If, from time to time,*
*we reflect on,*
*and accept,*
*the fact that our days are numbered*
*we are more likely to inhabit the earth*
*in a more loving, more responsible manner.*
*If we accept our own mortality,*
*we will find it easier*
*to love other people,*
*knowing that they, too,*
*have but a time to live*
*on the earth.*
*Indeed,*
*we're all in this together.*
*As the old saying has it,*
*no one gets out of here alive.*
*So,*
*the only sensible way to live*
*is with compassion,*
*forgiveness,*
*and tolerance.*

# A STRANGE SADNESS JOLTED ME AWAKE

Mary and her husband, Bud, had left his work on the Yakima Indian Reservation, in Washington state. The next year, they were living in Washington, D.C. Early one morning, Bud was in the kitchen making coffee while Mary caught a few more winks. Suddenly, Mary said, "I jolted awake with a strong feeling of sadness or dread. Something was wrong. I sat up and dialed my mother's number in Iowa. 'Are you all right?' I asked."

Mary's mother was fine. "Are you?" she responded. Child of the nineteenth century that she was, a long distance call could only be an emergency as far as she was concerned, especially one coming in the early morning.

Relieved, Mary told her mother of the feeling she had when she woke up so suddenly, and her mother reassured her. "She was fine, though startled to be awakened."

Mary hung up the phone, but the feeling of sadness and dread was still with her. Then, the phone rang.

"Latit?" the voice on the phone said, using the name Mary's Native American friends had given her. "It was the soft voice of my 'sister' on the Yakima Reservation," Mary said. The message: "Mom just passed away."

The woman who had died had been like a mother to Mary. She had taught Mary to twine, and she helped Bud—an agent with the U. S. Government's Bureau of Indian Affairs—learn what to do during longhouse ceremonies. She had honored Mary and Bud with Indian names, "so people will know you"—a reference, Mary said, "to the great hereafter."

Mary was left with a question in her mind. "Are the native people better able to send these messages than my non-Indian friends and relatives? Or was I more receptive that day? An Indian friend exhibited surprise, one time, when I hadn't known about a death...."

## Reflection

### Living Out of Touch

*Other cultures relate to death*
*more comfortably than does*
*the dominant American culture.*
*For other cultures,*
*death is a natural part of life,*
*nothing to be afraid of.*
*People in other cultures*
*often do not find it unusual at all*
*that communication should take place*
*between this world and the next.*
*We are so out of touch*
*with reality*
*that we find such communications astonishing.*
*We are so out of touch*
*with reality.*

# THE CLARITY AND WISDOM OF HEAVEN

Rosemary's friend, Sister Redempta, was a member of the Sisters of Mercy, a Catholic religious congregation, for sixty-one years. "Sister Redempta was an active member of the congregation until she drew her last breath," Rosemary said. "Redempta was a delight, a gentle soul, a woman of prayer her whole life through."

Sister Redempta died suddenly, and Rosemary was unable to attend the funeral service on June 25. "I woke early that morning," Rosemary said. "I slept on the sofa in the living room after spending a restless night in our bedroom. After waking, I closed my eyes again and the vision began. This was the first time I have ever had such an experience."

Rosemary saw Sister Redempta "looking through a wide panel of crystal-clear glass. The glass was invisible and yet I knew it was present. Instinctively, I realized she was seeing with the clarity and wisdom of heaven. The color tones were soft hues of gray.

"Then, I saw in the distance a wide vista of mountain range. A miraculous hand colored the mountains in the new green of eternal Spring. I saw the lines of a rainbow form and fill in with color.

"Sister Redempta turned toward me with her wise smile, she raised her arm and looked at her watch, tapped the face of the watch and looked at me. I had a keen awareness that time as we know it is short....

"There was one last scene. Redempta sat on a large sofa and gave to each member of New Bethlehem community—a small covenant community—a heart. (Members of this community exchanged paper hearts the previous February so that we each had a particular person to pray for.) Then in a gray mist she was gone."

## Reflection

### Living As a Reminder

*What do we think of people*
*who dedicate their lives to serving others and to prayer?*
*Do we think they are naive and unrealistic?*
*Do we shake our heads and think of them as deluded fools?*
*What do we think of people who do not marry,*
*who do not have children of their own,*
*so they may serve others*
*and spend more time in prayer?*
*Such people are a reminder*
*that nothing in this life*
*offers ultimate fulfillment*
*except love of God and neighbor.*
*It's as simple as that.*
*But maybe we do not wish to have*
*such a reminder.*

## "REPENT," HE SAID

Marie's husband died suddenly the day before his forty-first birthday. He had driven his and Marie's children to school while Marie worked in the family business. Sensing something was wrong, he drove himself to the doctor's office, but before the doctor could get him to the hospital he was dead. "I received a call from the physician," Marie said, "which I didn't believe because my husband was fine when I left. But it was true."

Marie's husband was a loving father and a devoted husband, and two weeks before he died he told Marie that he had never been happier.

"Shortly after his death," Marie recalled, "I was sleeping and saw him and spoke with him. He said that he was in purgatory and would be there for two years....He told me to repent for my sins."

Later, one evening after Marie's children were in bed, all the lights were off except for the room where Marie was watching television. Although she was absorbed in the program she was watching, something caught Marie's attention out of the corner of her eye, something in the dark dining room. "I could feel it coming towards me, and then my eyes filled with tears. I was not frightened, and then I knew that my husband was with us and watching over us."

Still later, Marie's oldest daughter brought home the picture taken at her high school prom. When Marie returned home that evening, she took the photographs to look at them. "I sensed something in back of me," she said, "and as I turned around my husband was standing there in a haze, as if to come over and look at the pictures because he was proud and loved his children very much, and then he disappeared."

Years went by, and Marie decided it was best to combine her home and business so she could be with her youngest daughter. She chose to move and build in another town. "I didn't know what would happen," she said, "whether my husband would come or stay with the house we had lived in together."

One of Marie's daughters followed in her father's occupation, and she won an award for her work. She was showing the medal to a customer one day. "My husband had been very active in starting a trade organization on a state level," Marie said, "and he was awarded a plaque with a clock. The clock was on the wall, but had not been wound for many years. As my daughter showed the medal she had won, the clock started ticking, and I felt that this was my husband's way of letting us know he was proud of her."

Not wishing to be thought unbalanced, Marie said nothing about these experiences, even to her children. Later, however, she learned that her children had similar experiences. "My middle daughter saw him in the living room while she was sitting at the desk," Marie said.

# Reflection

## Room for Improvement

*Catholicism*
*retains a belief in purgatory*
*while other Christian traditions have either rejected it*
*or feel ambivalent about it.*
*The Catholic conviction is*
*that hardly ever does anyone die*
*as a perfect person.*
*Each person has some faults,*
*some failings,*
*some sins*
*for which he or she,*
*and nobody else,*
*is responsible.*
*So it seems reasonable to suggest*
*that after death some form of purification*
*or refinement*
*would happen prior to one's entrance*
*into eternal bliss.*

*Regardless, the belief in purgatory*
*is about the next world, so it's simply*
*a reasonable guess.*
*If it has meaning for this life*
*it is that when it comes to the world*
*and all things human,*
*there is always room for improvement.*

# A DAUGHTER RETURNS

Elana was driving one day, with her son and fourteen-year-old daughter in the car, when their vehicle was struck by the vehicle of a drunk driver. "My first experience," Elana said, "was when she and I died at the same time. I traveled through a dark tunnel only to reach what I believed was heaven. I saw my daughter running ahead of me looking as if she had not a care in the world, unlike the troubles she had experienced on earth."

Initially, Elana couldn't understand why there was "so much bright light," but then her daughter stopped running, turned, and faced her mother, "and then I knew what had happened." Elana's daughter began to explain that "I was not to follow her as my time was not up yet but hers was." As Elana began to cry, her daughter said that she hoped Elana could forgive her for all the trouble she had caused, and she promised to work hard where she was going.

"At the moment she turned to go I thought I was calling after her, but I was telling the paramedics who had been successful in starting my heart that I couldn't breathe. They rescued my son and me after twenty minutes of being trapped in our car."

Six months later, Elana heard "noises" in her living room at 3 o'clock in the morning. She got out of bed to see what was going on but at first could see nothing out of the ordinary. "While I sat in the kitchen crying out for my daughter, trying to make sense of her death and of my life being spared, an angel appeared in front of me. The face was my daughter's but the body was ethereal. She began telling me how sad she felt because I was in so much pain, that my tears were not for her loss but for myself."

Elana's daughter then motioned for her to pick up a pen, and she wrote down the message of comfort and consolation that her daughter dictated. "She then floated up in the air, told me that she would always be with me, and how much she loved me, and then she was gone."

During the following three years Elana spoke at schools and colleges, sharing her story, and she "vowed to help make a difference, which I believe I have."

# Reflection

### Messages of Love

*Loved ones who have died,*
*then return to comfort and support those close to them*
*seem to "come back" in a variety of ways and forms.*
*The appearance of the one who "returns"*
*seems to have something with what will be*
*most meaningful*
*for the one to whom the deceased love one returns.*
*In the end, however,*
*the form matters little.*
*What matters is the fact that the loved one*
*returns with a message of love and encouragement*
*and the message that*
*there is nothing to worry about.*
*This, of course, is one of the main themes*
*of the Gospels:*
*there is no need to worry or be anxious.*
*Jesus says it time and time again*
*in the Gospels.*

# "IT'S OKAY, BABE"

In the first weeks after her husband's death, Sara was "in shock." Then one night, three months later, "the reality finally hit me," she said. "I lay on my bed and cried and cried." Finally, she got ready for bed, feeling "very restless."

Then, Sara said, she felt her husband kiss her on the cheek, and he said, "It's okay, Babe." Immediately, Sara fell into "a very sound and peaceful sleep. I know this was not a dream."

## Reflection

### This Life Is Trustworthy

*Theologians suggest that what we are,*
*we human beings,*
*is embodied spirits.*
*So important is our bodiliness*
*that it can be a wrenching experience*
*when confronted by the death of a*
*relative or friend.*
*The person seems to be*
*completely gone*
*because his or her bodiliness*
*has ceased to be lively.*
*More to the point, we may find it difficult*
*to find the same meaning in life*
*without the person who was there before.*
*It's nice to get a message*
*from beyond*
*that this life remains meaningful*
*and trustworthy,*
*even after death seems to deprive us*
*of a person we love.*

# "CALL UNCLE CHARLES"

Peggy's mother died leaving her alone at the age of eighteen. Her father had died earlier, and Peggy was an only child. An uncle and aunt who lived nearby invited Peggy to stay with them, but she chose to live alone so she could be near her boyfriend.

"We became engaged to be married," Peggy said, "and had our wedding planned, when everything fell apart. I was overcome with grief and did not know where to turn."

One afternoon as Peggy drove along in her car, she was crying and thinking of her mother and how much she missed her support. "I felt her say to me, 'Call Uncle Charles.' I had no doubt that she was present and reminding me that she had asked her brother, my godfather, to look out for me."

Peggy was too upset to call and explain everything to her uncle, since he knew nothing of her predicament. So, she went home and wrote everything in a letter to her uncle and aunt, asking if she could live with them until she got over her broken engagement. "On receiving my letter," Peggy said, "my aunt called immediately to invite me to come, and I did go to live with them for one year.

"My mom was there for me even after her death."

# Reflection

### Acting for Others

*That great, often-quoted author,*
*Anonymous, once said:*
*"Our lives are a manifestation*
*of what we think about God."*
*If we believe in a loving, compassionate God,*
*we will expect others to act in a loving, compassionate manner,*
*and we will be inclined to act in the same manner.*

*When a young relative calls*
*needing someplace to live for a while,*
*we will take her in.*
*Over and over,*
*communications from deceased loved ones*
*remind us of how we should live.*

# WHITE CLOUDS
# IN THE LIVING ROOM

Nancy once had a professional astrologer draw up her personal astrological chart based on her birth date. The astrologer told her that she would experience spiritual phenomena and that she was destined "for big things."

Nancy had heard about "ghosts, vapors, and poltergeists," but she never believed in such things until an experience she had after the sudden death of her husband, John, at age fifty.

About three weeks after her husband's death, Nancy was sitting in her living room watching the evening news. "Suddenly, what appeared to be a white cloud went gracefully floating through the living room and into the dining room, about a foot from the ceiling, and disappeared through the wall! I could hardly believe my eyes."

That same night, Nancy, a Catholic, went to bed early and began to pray the rosary for the repose of her husband's soul. "Sure enough," she said, "that same little white cloud or spirit came sailing through the bedroom and disappeared through the window. Needless to say, I was scared and all alone. I buried my head under the covers and went to sleep."

The next day, Nancy called a tearoom in a nearby city where people go to have tea leaves and Tarot cards read, and for psychic readings. Nancy told her story to the woman who answered the phone, and the woman asked if anyone close to her had died recently. "I told her yes, my husband died of a heart attack quite suddenly about three weeks ago."

The woman at the tearoom told Nancy not to worry, that the "white cloud or spirit" was not a bad omen, and her house was not haunted. Rather, her husband's spirit was "earth bound," and he was concerned about how Nancy was getting along without him.

Later that week, after supper, Nancy stood at her kitchen sink washing dishes. She heard "a loud knocking on the refrigerator." Nancy's husband had loved to cook, prepare meals, and shop for food. "I really felt his presence around me," she said, "and I heard a snapping sound going through the house. I said out loud, 'Oh John, I miss you so much!'"

Another evening, Nancy stood waiting for the bus she took home from work. "Suddenly, I saw my husband's ghost on the opposite side of the subway waiting to board the train for Boston. He had on his old slacks, jacket, and hat, as well as his eye glasses, and he was smoking his pipe!"

Nancy was shocked. "I wanted to yell over to him or tell the lady next to me, 'There's my husband, and he died a month ago!' She would have said, 'Lady, you are crazy!' However, I kept it to myself."

A few days later, Nancy went to shop for groceries when she saw her husband again. "This time he was all dressed up in his best clothes and walking very fast ahead of me. I ran to catch up with him, and when I got into the market he was nowhere to be seen."

Nancy's husband died, and nine years later she moved from the suburbs into the city where she finds it more convenient to live in a senior citizen apartment house. A man who lived on the same floor as Nancy, two doors down from her, had cancer, and one Christmas season by his door she left a bag of "popcorn, goodies and a Christmas card." The card read, "Just a little something for you to munch on while you are watching your favorite videos," and, Nancy said, "I wished him a Merry Christmas and a Healthy and Happy New Year."

Nancy's neighbor died after Christmas, and she never saw him again. About a month after his death, however, one night she went out into the corridor about midnight to empty some trash. "I noticed a lot of vapor outside of his apartment. I looked up at the top of it and saw his smiling face looking down at me. I got nervous and hurried into my apartment."

After so many years, Nancy still feels her husband's presence around her, in particular she says, "when I'm paying the bills, trying to balance the check book, or preparing my income tax return. It is a comforting feeling, and I find myself reading more books about 'life after life.'"

# Reflection

### Life Is So Worth Living

*This life is so worth living*
*that sometimes, it seems,*
*even those who have died*
*come back to be present in time.*
*What makes this life,*
*for all its troubles and trials,*
*so worth living?*
*The great seventeenth-century English poet,*
*John Donne, wrote:*
*"I count all that part of my life lost*
*which I spent not in communion with God*
*or in doing good."*

# AN APPARITION ABOVE THE TREES

Sister Mary, a Roman Catholic nun, said that her sister, Julia, died. "I miss her very much," Sister Mary said.

A few years later, in a dream Sister Mary saw Julia "above the trees clad in her military uniform and smiling beautifully." Julia had served in the Army Air Corps in World War II. "When I awoke I felt very much consoled and comforted," Sister Mary said.

# Reflection

## Reminders From God

*Why do deceased loved ones*
*often appear to us attired nattily*
*in clothing they wore in this life?*
*Perhaps this is but one more way*
*for God to say to us*
*that even the details of life in this world*
*are of some consequence.*
*Perhaps this is but one more way*
*for God to say to us*
*that we should enjoy even little things*
*like the clothes we wear.*
*It may also be a way to remind us that*
*we need to be concerned for those*
*who don't have the clothing they need.*

# "SHE LOVED CHILDREN"

When she was growing up, Geraldine's family lived in a big house with two other families. "An Italian aunt on the first floor, another on the second, and we were in the so-called attic apartment," she recalled. "My Aunt Anna Maria had no children of her own, but she loved children."

Geraldine was one of Aunt Anna Maria's favorite nieces. "I could tell she really loved me," Geraldine said. "She died many years ago, a victim of cancer. In life she always gave of herself. She was very sick with cancer but she came to my home to give me money to add on rooms to my house."

Aunt Anna Maria was godmother to Cindy, one of Geraldine's eight children. "She gave me the money to buy a beautiful dress and veil for Cindy's first holy Communion. When my youngest daughter's turn came, I searched the house for Cindy's outfit. I could not find it."

As the day drew closer, Geraldine became a little worried. Where was that dress? Then one night, she had a dream in which her aunt told her that the dress was in a box with blue paper in it on the first shelf in a particular closet. "In the morning, I looked," Geraldine said, "and sure enough there was the dress and veil just like Aunt Anna said in the dream. I actually saw the box, shelf, and closet, all in the dream. My aunt had died years ago but her spirit is very much alive.

"People should be more like their ancestors," Geraldine continued, "who were giving to people, doing for others. My memories of my aunt will never fade away. I know she is up in heaven praying for us."

# Reflection

## Doing Good

*There are do-gooders,*
*and good doers.*
*Mrs. Jellyby, in Dickens' novel,* Bleak House,
*is a do-gooder.*
*She constantly dashes about*
*doing good for the natives*
*"on the banks of the Niger*
*in Borrioboolagah."*
*At the same time,*
*her own husband and her many children*
*are neglected, hungry, and ill-clad.*
*Good doers, on the other hand,*
*are like the woman who, though dying,*
*goes to visit a relative to give her money.*
*Many are the people who wouldn't think of*
*giving money away,*
*not even if they are dying.*

# A MOTHER'S HUG

Kathy's mother died at the age of fifty-four. She and Kathy were very close, and Kathy was her mother's only child. "I was absolutely devastated by her death, and although I'm much better now, it's still hard to take sometimes," she said.

Later, for the third consecutive year Kathy participated in a silent retreat for women, and she did not know any of the other women there. In the course of the retreat, a healing service was offered for those on retreat. "For the first time in three years of attending this retreat," she said, "I did not pray for healing regarding the feelings of loss I felt for my mother. I really had been feeling as if I was finally getting on with my life, and I wasn't feeling the pangs of loss as acutely as I had been for the first year or so after Mom's death."

After the group prayed the Our Father, they were invited to share a sign of peace with one another. Since she didn't know anyone there very well, Kathy simply exchanged pleasantries with those she greeted. Then, a woman approached and said, "You look like you could use a mother's hug."

Kathy replied, "Yes, I guess I could," and she and the other woman embraced. "It took a few minutes before all this sunk in," she said. "I thought to myself, yes, I could have used a mother's hug for about three years now." This experience was especially meaningful to Kathy, because just before her mother died she gave Kathy a big hug, even though normally she wasn't a very demonstrative person.

After the woman gave Kathy "a mother's hug," Kathy said she was "in tears and sobbing for the next couple of hours. I really felt good afterwards, though, like I could really feel my mother's presence. I felt thoroughly cleansed, too, after this experience. I guess that I really did need more healing regarding my mother's death, although I didn't realize it before. Or maybe I knew it but didn't want to acknowledge it."

During the dinner at the end of the retreat, Kathy exchanged addresses with the woman who gave her "a mother's hug," and she told her about her mother. "She was flabbergasted and got quite emotional herself," Kathy said. "She told me that she had been watching me during the retreat and said that I just looked like I needed a mother's hug. That's the image that came to mind, and she was moved to express that during the healing service."

This experience, Kathy said, made her feel the nearness of her mother, "like she really wanted to bodily touch me one more time and was able to do so through this woman. The experience definitely made a difference to me. It made me feel the nearness of my mother and gave me a hope-filled feeling that Mom does still exist. I believe and have always believed that there is an afterlife, but when you lose someone very close to you those beliefs are challenged. This experience reaffirmed my faith that this is a life after death and that Mom was doing fine and letting me know that she was there."

A year later, on the anniversary of her mother's death, Kathy came home from work to find in her mail box an envelope from her new friend. "I was feeling kind of down, like I usually do on Mom's anniversary date. When I opened it, all the card said was something like, 'Just writing to say "hi," and sending you love and a big hug.' Well, here came the tears again. I once again really felt Mom's presence. It's like she's trying to remind me that she isn't really all that far away, she's still watching out for me and wants me to remember that she loves me. That's the only explanation that I could possibly have for all of this. These experiences have truly been blessings in my life and have helped me to heal even more thoroughly."

# Reflection

### Being There for One Another

*When a person we love dies*
*there is bound to be a wound*
*—spiritual and emotional—*
*that must heal.*

*We can't count on the one we loved*
*coming back to us*
*in some remarkable manner*
*to help us feel better.*
*Most of the time*
*this does not happen.*
*We who share this good life,*
*however, can be there*
*for one another,*
*to support, encourage, and love.*

# THE MUSIC GOES ON

In his biography of jazz great Miles Davis, *So What: The Life of Miles Davis* (Simon & Schuster, 2002), author John Szwed writes matter-of-factly:

> Miles' death [in 1990] affected many people deeply, sometimes even spiritually. Irene [former wife] said that "when Miles passed, he came to me. He appeared on the TV and said, 'Come on, I'll take you home.' I said, 'Miles, aren't you supposed to be dead?'..." Miles also appeared to [artist and friend] Jackie Battle, but in a dream a week before he died: he hugged her and said goodbye.

## Reflection

### Time and Space Intersects

*Is it too weird that someone would appear,*
*after death,*
*via a television broadcast?*
*Does it mix up time and space*
*beyond comprehension*

*to the point of boggling the mind*
*that someone who has not yet died*
*would visit a friend in a dream*
*to say goodbye*
*even before he or she has died?*
*Remember, however,*
*that death is the intersection between*
*time/space and the mystery we call*
*eternity.*
*Who's to say what's weird*
*and what's not weird?*

# ONE BLAST OF LOVE

Nina Polcyn Moore, a longtime friend of Dorothy Day and the Catholic Worker movement, contributed a clipping from an issue of *The Catholic Worker* newspaper. Author Jack McMurry described the death of his wife, Susie, from malignant melanoma. Susie was one of the grandchildren of Dorothy Day, the cofounder of the Catholic Worker movement.

"More and more," Jack wrote, "I learned to relate to Susie's spirit, not her body, knowing that this ravaged body was not the woman I loved. What I loved was an essence that was trapped inside this body, an essence untouched by cancer, immortal, indestructible. I could sense her spirit waiting for this drama to end so it could move on to other adventures in the universe."

Susie made it easy for Jack and their three daughters. "She never complained, her greatest concern was for the kids...and for me. She instructed her children well on what was happening, and what was going to happen. Susie could not expel the melanoma from her home, but she did expel fear and ignorance. She left us in a state of peace and wonderment."

During Susie's last three days, she was in a coma. "Her heart beat was almost double, and her breathing was very rapid, like a runner's. She was on the runway. Her breathing stopped on a quiet Sunday afternoon. When Susie's spirit finally freed itself from her body, a great energy filled the room. It seemed to make the walls bulge out. We became engulfed in a vibration of great peace and love. It was the most holy moment of my life. It was love coming to a full cycle. I felt blessed and honored by this experience. It was Susie's way of saying, thank you, it's okay now. One blast of love before moving on."

# Reflection

## Our Love for One Another

*What is love?*
*We live in a culture that uses the word "love"*
*in many ways,*
*some of them superficial and self-centered,*
*some of them unrealistically romantic.*
*Love, said Saint Thomas Aquinas,*
*in the thirteenth century,*
*is to will the good of the other.*
*This is what God does for us,*
*and this is what we are to do for one another.*
*Sometimes when a person dies,*
*those present experience*
*the good and power*
*of the dying person's love for them.*
*It is quite astonishing to realize that*
*the love we have for one another*
*has this same goodness and power.*
*Most of the time,*
*it doesn't show.*
*But it's there all the same.*

# HAPPY PEOPLE

Shortly after the death of her father, Sister Louise, a Roman Catholic nun, had a vivid dream. "I saw my father surrounded by a group of very happy and radiant people. My father also looked very happy, and I would say his face was radiant with joy. When I saw my father, I ran to him and threw myself into his arms, begging to be allowed to stay with him. He, however, still smiling, told me that I could not stay with him just then, but that he would always watch over me and would be waiting for me when I could be with him. With that, I awoke with a feeling of deep peace and joy replacing the sadness and anguish that had filled my heart after my father's very sudden death."

Following the death of a favorite aunt, Sister Louise had another dream. "My aunt and I were standing on a platform awaiting a train. When the train arrived, my aunt got on it, but just as I was about to do the same, the door closed and the train pulled away. I began running down the platform trying to catch the train. My aunt appeared at a back window and, looking very happy, told me not to run after the train. She told me I need not worry or be sad because we would meet again. I again awoke feeling very happy and at peace."

Sister Louise said that the memory of these two dreams "still makes me feel happy after all these years."

## Reflection

### Divisions in This Life Can Be Healed

*Death causes divisions.*
*We are separated from ones that we love.*
*But the division caused by death*
*is only apparent.*
*Its reality is superficial*
*because the deceased person*

*is still with us, closer than before.*
*The divisions we should be more concerned about*
*are divisions that happen in this world.*
*Divisions based on hatred, prejudice,*
*and injustice.*
*We can do nothing about*
*the apparent divisions caused by death.*
*But we can do something about the divisions*
*between people in this life*
*caused by sheer meanness.*

# "WHO'S THAT MAN?"

Ann was the fourth child in a family of five. "I wasn't the first one to break curfews or try to stretch rules," she said, "so my relationship with my parents was never strained. I believe I was my father's favorite child. We shared a special rapport. Our minds were in synch, perhaps because he was a real hero to me, and I began to emulate his actions and words."

When Ann's father died at age sixty-seven, it was a crushing blow to her. She felt numb, hollow, "as if every nerve end had been repeatedly beaten." She cried a great deal, feeling that her heart was broken.

At the time, Ann's son was six and-a-half years old, and he has always been sensitive to the moods of others. As Ann lay in bed one night wishing her father was still alive, she saw "in a dark corner of the room the shadowy shape of a man."

Ann knew the shape was her father, but she thought perhaps she was seeing an illusion created by her mind because she was in so much pain at his loss. "My son stumbled into the bedroom saying that he wanted to crawl into bed with my husband and myself. I held back the covers, and as he got into bed he said, 'Mom, who's that man standing in the corner?' I told him, 'Grandpa,' and we were both comforted."

# Reflection

### Life Is a Mixed Bag

*Over and over again,*
*come stories of deceased relatives and friends*
*who return, in some form,*
*with the same message:*
*that they are not really gone,*
*just present in another way.*
*Over and over again,*
*we are reassured by these experiences*
*and these stories.*
*Why do we find so much comfort*
*in these experiences and stories?*
*Perhaps it's because*
*life is such a mixed bag.*
*Amid all the light*
*there is so much darkness.*
*In the midst of our belief*
*there is so much unbelief.*
*So, when something out of the ordinary happens,*
*some event that brings reassurance*
*that our faith is trustworthy*
*we welcome it with all our heart.*
*But the lesson is the same,*
*time after time:*
*ultimately,*
*everything is going to be okay.*

# NOTHING CAN COMPARE—NOTHING

Mary's late aunt, Margaret, shared Mary's home with her for ten years. Margaret died of respiratory arrest, in a nursing home at the age of eighty-six. "She fell asleep," Mary said, "and awakened in heaven."

One day a few months later, Mary said, "I sensed her presence in my living room and heard her voice in my heart clearly saying, "There's nothing there to compare to here—nothing."

A year or two later, Mary heard Margaret say, "I didn't know you'd had so much sadness."

## Reflection

**Our Ultimate Destiny**

*As long as we are in this life*
*our focus should be on this life.*
*To become preoccupied with*
*the next life*
*is to neglect what we are meant to be about*
*now.*
*Still, this life will come to an end*
*one day,*
*and ultimately we are meant*
*for a better life.*
*So it's natural to be curious*
*about what comes next.*
*There is no need to be afraid*
*about that.*
*It's as simple as that.*
*Now get on with the tasks at hand,*
*and do them with love.*

# THE PATIO BELL

Patricia's sister brought her a patio bell from Arizona. "It had a special place on our patio, and it meant a lot to me," Patricia said. A few years later, Patricia's sister died of cancer. "We had hoped that she would recover but a heart attack quickly took her."

A few days following the funeral, Patricia sat on her patio feeling very sad, missing her sister. "It was a still day with no wind," she recalled, "and suddenly the bell started to chime. I felt elated as I took it as a sign from her that she was still with me. I told her that whenever I heard the bell I would say an Our Father, Hail Mary, and Glory Be for the poor souls in purgatory. It reminds me quite often to do just that."

Patricia said that this experience has helped her through the grieving process and is a special way of communicating with her sister.

## Reflection

**Prayer Changes Us**

*If we, or others,*
*experience the presence of a deceased relative or friend,*
*that experience will bear much fruit*
*if it encourages us to be more faithful in prayer.*
*Søren Kierkegaard,*
*the early nineteenth-century Danish Christian philosopher,*
*said:*
*"Prayer does not change God,*
*but changes him who prays."*
*Maybe that is one reason we are sometimes*
*reluctant to pray.*
*We are satisfied with ourselves*
*just the way we are,*
*thank you very much.*

# A CHAIR FOR THE SPIRIT

A young Roman Catholic nun, Sister Kathy, succumbed after a four-year battle with cancer. Her friend, Kathleen, was a lay eucharistic minister in her parish, and on Holy Thursday she was scheduled to minister at the evening service.

"There was an empty chair next to me in the sanctuary," Kathleen recalled, "and at some point during the service I really felt like Sister Kathy's spirit was sitting in that chair next to me."

The same experience has happened to Kathleen on other occasions, when she was part of the congregation during the Mass. "Seated in a pew by myself, all of a sudden it felt like Kathy was standing in the pew next to me. It's always a peaceful feeling when it has happened."

Kathleen has also had a recurring dream in which Sister Kathy is seated in a garden. "I come along and we sit and chat. She always has to leave first and says to me, 'You can't come with me this time, but someday you will be able to.'"

Another nun friend interpreted Kathleen's dream to mean that Sister Kathy is going back to heaven but it's not Kathleen's time follow her, although someday it will be.

"I consider Kathy to be a saint," Kathleen said, "and I do pray to her. One of her family members told me of similar experiences they have had with Kathy's spirit."

## Reflection

**Ready for Death**

*How many times have you celebrated*
*your birthday?*
*That same number of times*
*(unless your birthday is February 29!)*
*you have lived the date on the calendar*
*on which you will die.*

*We know when our birthday is,*
*but we don't know when our deathday is.*
*But the day is coming*
*when we will die.*
*Sometimes, if we long to be*
*with loved ones who have died,*
*they tell us that we must stay where we are*
*for now,*
*but often they add that someday*
*we will join them.*
*Rather than being frightened by*
*our mortality,*
*we should rejoice in it,*
*living each day to the fullest,*
*but prepared to pass over*
*the Great Divide*
*whenever our deathday may come.*
*Doing it all, believe it or not,*
*with joy.*

# GOOSE BUMPS GALORE

When Anne got married, she accepted the responsibilities that come with a husband and family. What she hadn't counted on was "a real, live, inherited hermit uncle."

Basically, Uncle Ed was a good soul, Anne said, but either he had turned sour on life or life had turned sour on him. "To say he was unkempt is surely an understatement. His physical state went beyond mere neglect. If his teeth posed a problem, he pulled them. If his hair became too long, he cut it. These were minor traits, and I'm sure they could have been tolerated if he hadn't had such a strong aversion to soap and water. After one of his visits, days passed before the sweet essence of his presence disappeared."

Uncle Ed was small in stature, a little over five feet, but his width was something else, Ann explained. "He was as wide as he was tall. His face was unforgettable, with a huge hook nose and a large blue mole housed on the very end. His face was pitted with blackheads from years of neglect. It was common knowledge that he lived in a one-room shack without any of the conveniences of a modern home."

After Ed's sister—Anne's mother-in-law—passed away, Uncle Ed "adopted" Anne's family. "With the appearance of Easter lilies, daffodils, and narcissus in the supermarkets and flower shops," she recalled, "we could be sure Uncle Ed's old car would pull up and park under the maples at the front of the house."

Easter wasn't the only holiday that would whistle up Uncle Ed's presence. "When March and April slipped by, there he would be approaching the front door, suitcase in hand, all ready for the Memorial Day parade."

No sooner had Uncle Ed departed than the Fourth of July would be upon Anne and her family, and here came Uncle Ed for another visit of at least two weeks. "With the first week of September and Labor Day, back he came again!"

Another two months went by, the leaves changed color and fell, and snow covered the sidewalks and window sills. "Inside, the house was polished for Thanksgiving and Christmas—and the arrival of Uncle Ed."

At times, Uncle Ed could irritate the mightiest archangel, Anne said, "but he had wormed his way into our life, and with each approaching holiday I waited expectantly for his arrival. Year after year, with each changing season, the same routine was followed, and he always arrived on schedule."

Uncle Ed watched Anne's older children grow from babies to young ladies. "Perhaps," she suggested, "he visualized them as the family he had never had. My family increased in size, but this never deterred Uncle Ed's arrival. Regardless of the situation, arrive he did, and we made a bed available for him."

Uncle Ed was an unselfish individual, Anne said, one who was always doing for others. "One winter he built me a knotty pine kitchen. He could do anything, including building a whole house.

One time he told me his dead mother called his name to awaken him before he was overcome by carbon monoxide fumes."

The years flew by, as years have a way of doing when you're busy raising a family, and there came a Fourth of July when Uncle Ed appeared after being absent for a whole year. "One look at the pallored face, the jaundiced eyes, and the curled, drooping, lop-sided mouth, and it was obvious the poor old man had suffered a stroke. Having little faith in doctors, or perhaps having no means to put himself in their care, he refrained from seeking help, but he felt in his heart he was on the mend."

In the company of Anne and her family, Uncle Ed spent the long, humid July afternoons sitting in the yard in the shade of the trees. His mind went back to events of almost eighty years ago. "The farther back he went with the story," Anne said, "the more lucid the account. The more recent the event, the more vague and incoherent he became."

Finally, Uncle Ed's visit came to an end, and his talk centered on when and if he would return. "We said our goodbyes, neither of us realizing it was our last earthly meeting."

September came, followed by Thanksgiving and Christmas, but no Uncle Ed. "His time for visiting had ended," Anne said. "I did receive a thoughtful letter at Christmas time. He wrote of his desire to be with us and wished us a joyous Christmas and New Year."

With the ice- and snowbound days of January came word that Uncle Ed had died. "He had dropped while shoveling snow. The winter day he was buried, relatives gathered after the funeral at the home of a cousin. "While there, we visited, reminisced, lunched, and finally dispersed. That night, Uncle Ed said his goodbye as surely as if he had appeared."

All was quiet in Anne's house. "The children had all fallen asleep," she remembered, "as I wearily sat on the edge of my bed. I pulled my dress over my head and laid it on the bed beside me before bending over to remove my shoes and socks. Suddenly, I felt a light touch on my shoulder. Turning my head from side to side, I looked over my shoulder. No one was there. I sat there staring blankly ahead while my brain tried to comprehend what my sixth sense accepted. Uncle Ed had said his goodbye."

Anne's story might have ended there if it were not for one more remarkable experience.

In the first months following Uncle Ed's death, with the approach of a holiday he would be in her thoughts. As the months passed, however, this happened less frequently. "The children grew, and we moved out of the old house in the country to a new house in the village. I thought how much Uncle Ed would have enjoyed our new home. Then I forgot him completely in the whirl of life. He was all but forgotten until my oldest daughter's wedding day approached."

As the day for the wedding drew near, Anne spoke of Uncle Ed. He had watched this daughter grow who was about to be married, and such a day would have held a special place in his heart. Then, something unexplainable happened.

At this time, Anne worked in a soup-and-sandwich shop close to a motel. One week before her daughter's wedding, she placed a menu and glass of water in front of an elderly gentleman seated in one of the booths she was responsible for. "I quietly took his order," Anne said, "brought his hot soup and crackers, and placed his sandwich order. Then I stood waiting for the inevitable noon-hour rush."

Business was slow for the moment, however, and when Anne delivered the old man's sandwich he drew her into conversation. "I clearly recall there was a certain familiarity in his appearance," Anne said. "His nose was quite prominent, his skin a deathly pasty white. I wondered to myself if he suffered from leukemia."

Briefly, the man gave Anne a few details about his life. He was a bachelor, and his doctor had told him his time on earth was rapidly coming to a close. Anne listened attentively while he told her of his life. Then he spoke of his favorite pastime, writing poetry. She asked if his poems had ever been published. He laughed quietly and said, "No." He claimed to have written twelve hundred poems, then he promised to write one especially for Anne.

The shop began to fill with the noontime crowd, and in the

hustle and bustle of filling orders the old man left unnoticed by Anne. Late that afternoon, however, as she prepared to leave for home, one of the other waitresses pushed open the door to the back room and handed her a folder paper. She said that an elderly man asked her to deliver it to Anne.

On a folded sheet of motel stationery was a poem about the real meaning of life:

**Just Me**

I've climbed nearly to the top,
And the bottom I've also seen
But I'd really like to end up
Just halfway in between.

It's nice to be a big shot
And think you're someone big,
But to me it doesn't matter
If I'm a tree or just a twig.

If you love the world you live in
And the people you chance to meet
You will never have a lonely hour,
When walking down the street.

So face tomorrow with a smile,
Make friends as you go along,
Don't carry a chip on your shoulder,
But in your heart a song.

Anne said that she read through the poem twice, thinking what a beautiful sentiment it carried from a man who was dying. "Then," she added, "goose bumps crawled up my back and over my arms. Little shivers made my body quiver as I stood there alone." The signature at the bottom of the poem read, "Your friend always, Ed."

"I have always felt," Anne said, "that the strange old man

who wrote the poem was Uncle Ed. I even compared the signature at the bottom of the poem, and it certainly resembles Uncle Ed's."

# Reflection

**Peculiar But Holy**

*Hey, Ed!*
*One of your poems*
*has been published!*
*In a song titled, "Friend of Jesus,"*
*contemporary American singer-song writer, John Stewart,*
*wrote:*
*"Jesus hung with the hardline gang.*
*Jesus knew the songs they sang.*
*He didn't have no money,*
*I hear he didn't have a dime.*
*I do believe I'd've been a friend*
*of Jesus in his time."*
*Sometimes to be around the odd ducks of the world*
*is to find yourself close to*
*a very peculiar holiness,*
*the sacred in some very off-beat forms.*
*Peculiar and off-beat,*
*but holy all the same.*

# "HIS WAY OF REASSURING ME"

One of the more unusual accounts of a communication with a deceased loved one is in *Messages and Miracles*, by Louis E. LaGrand, Ph.D. (Llewellyn Publications, 1999). Edna explains that she was praying the Rosary one morning before leaving for work, praying the Sorrowful Mysteries. The Rosary devotional booklet Edna was using suggested, "Ask Him to be with you at the hour of your death.'" "I said, 'God please be with me and let my husband be there to help me make my transition. Let him be there waiting for me.' As I said this, the lights in the kitchen (which were on) went off and on a couple of times and finally stayed on. This startled me and I looked up and said, 'Hon, is that you? Are you letting me know that you're here with me? Thank you.' I decided to check the microwave because had it been a power surge the light on the microwave would have gone off. It hadn't. It was 7:53 A.M."

Edna interpreted her experience as a communication from her late husband reassuring her that he would be there waiting for her when her time came to die. "This experience certainly helped me with my grief. It allows me to continue believing that someday my husband and I will be together once more.... Knowing that I'll see him again makes life a little easier for me now."

# Reflection

### No Limits

*Who knows why some who have*
*passed over*
*communicate with us in one way,*
*others in other ways?*
*Are lights blinking on and off*
*at an opportune moment*
*a mere coincidence?*
*Maybe.*
*But maybe, by golly, maybe not.*
*Who can really tell?*
*Are we ready to place limits*
*on how deceased loved ones*
*can communicate with us?*

# AN EGG WITH A DIFFERENCE

Lena had a little sister who had a beautiful brown chicken which followed her everywhere she went. "That hen was her pet and played with her like a little puppy."

Lena's sister was a victim of pneumonia, however, and died at eighteen months of age. "Beginning the day of her funeral," Lena recalled, "this hen laid two eggs a day, and on the seventh day she laid one with a cross on it. At first my dad thought it was the imprint of a chicken's foot, but no, it was a perfect cross. The harder my dad rubbed the egg the brighter the cross became. He took the egg to our priest and he could hardly believe it. He was astonished and told my dad to take the egg to our daily newspaper."

As Lena's father was on his way to the newspaper's office, he stopped by the house before going into town. He had blown the egg out of the shell and filled it with sand, and now it was in his jacket pocket. As he took off his jacket the pocket with the egg in it struck a nearby sewing machine and broke.

The seventh day after Lena's little sister's funeral, the chicken quit laying eggs and ran around apparently looking for her lost playmate. "She died about a month later," Lena said.

## Reflection

**Quality Control**

*Stranger things have happened.*
*Some stories are loaded with goodness and humanity.*
*Some stories are such good, simple stories*
*that they need no commentary.*
*Some stories come from a time*
*most people today never experienced,*
*when almost all families lived on farms,*
*and a little girl might have a pet chicken,*
*or a pet goat, or a pet pig.*

*Some stories come from a time,*
*once upon a time*
*in real time,*
*when a chicken might lay an egg*
*with a cross on it.*
*Nowadays, such an egg*
*would never make it to the supermarket.*
*Quality control,*
*you know.*

# "GO BACK, IT'S BURNING"

In a dream, Irving and his wife, Cornelia, were on their way to take the ferry from Oakland, California, to San Francisco. "Irving's brother, Jack, had died of heart disease some years before," Cornelia said, "but in the dream he came in and sat down next to Irving and said, 'Go back, it's burning.'"

Cornelia and Irving had planned to take the ferry to San Francisco the next day, but when he awoke and told her about his dream, it was so real he couldn't bring himself to make the trip. "That evening," Cornelia said, "in the newspaper there was a big spread about the fire on the ferry, how the ferry just made it to the slip and they got the passengers off. But in the meantime the slip caught fire and the whole place was burned out. They had a picture of the ruins with the article."

## Reflection

### Asking for Help

*What happens in this life is significant.*
*Our interests, welfare, and concerns*
*are significant not only in this world*
*but in the eternal realm.*

*Yet how often do we turn*
*to the Divine Mystery we call*
*God,*
*or to someone who dwells there now—*
*someone we knew, perhaps,*
*or some saint—*
*to ask for intercession with God?*
*Do we not ask*
*because we don't actually believe*
*in such things?*

# "THE BEST NIGHT'S SLEEP I EVER HAD"

Joan's mother died. "I only got to see her once before she died," Joan said, "because the next day I became sick and wasn't allowed to see her."

Following her mother's death, Joan prayed that she might see her mother one more time. "About two weeks later, I was sleeping and I dreamed my mother died. When I went to see her, she woke up, took a shower, and got dressed. I ran downstairs to tell my sister that our mother was still alive and that she didn't die."

Joan and her mother often went to see movies together. In the dream, after Joan's mother got dressed, she told Joan she wanted to go to the movies. "As we were walking, she kept patting me on my face and arms, and on the way out of the movie house, she told me she had to use the ladies room, and I should go home, she would see me there later. I started to walk, and then I stopped and ran back to find her, but she wasn't there. I said to myself that she really did die, and when I got home I told my sister."

"The point is this," Joan concluded. "That was the best night's sleep I have ever had in my life. It was the most peaceful, relaxing sleep. I was smiling, happy, and very peaceful all day the next day, and I wished it would have lasted longer."

# Reflection

**Learning to Trust**

*The sacred writings*
*of many religious traditions*
*encourage us to give up*
*worry and anxiety.*
*In the Gospels, for example,*
*Jesus admonishes his disciples*
*time and time again*
*to stop worrying.*
*We are meant to be at peace,*
*but daily we choose anxiety instead.*
*In order to be at peace,*
*we must choose to trust,*
*to place our worries and concerns*
*with the One who is ultimately worthy of trust.*

# "I EXPERIENCED A DEEP PEACE AND JOY"

Sister M. Madeleine, a Roman Catholic nun, said that her brother, Jerome, was mentally ill and an alcoholic, "after a life beset for the most part by many trials and hardships." Jerome died at the age of fifty-six.

"When I last visited him," Sister M. Madeline said, "I found him sad and lonely, yet strangely less bitter and depressed. "Two weeks later, Jerome accidentally fell and was found dead from the resulting head injuries.

"My sorrow over this sudden and unprepared death was further compounded by the image of his sad and dejected countenance," Sister M. Madeline said, "and I prayed for him all the more."

Two years after Jerome's death, Sister M. Madeline was making a retreat. "I asked the retreat director to offer Mass for Jerome." During the Mass, when the priest said, "Let us pray for Jerome for whom this Mass is being offered," something astonishing happened.

"Jerome's face, radiant with joy and beaming with a light I cannot describe, became present to me," Sister M. Madeline said. "I experienced a deep peace and joy. My brother, I think, was telling me he was at peace and not to be concerned about him."

# Reflection

### Care for the Downtrodden

*Some people,*
*for reasons perplexing,*
*have lives loaded with misfortune*
*and sadness.*
*An old folk spiritual says:*
*"Nobody knows*
*the trouble I've seen,*
*nobody knows but Jesus."*
*Death, for such people,*
*can seem to be a particular blessing.*
*While they are with us, however,*
*we are called to care for them*
*as best we can*
*and pray for them.*

# WITH MY MOTHER
# IN GOD'S PRESENCE

The mother of Sister M. Madeline was dying. "My heart was broken at the thought that soon she would leave us," she said. "I was praying for her."

At the moment of her mother's last breath, however, something happened. "I suddenly experienced the greatest sense of elation and joy, a feeling never before felt as I stood there with my mother in God's Presence."

## Reflection

### In and Out of Time

*The moment of death*
*is a moment when time and eternity intersect.*
*The moment of death is a moment*
*in and out of time.*
*The moment of death is holy,*
*even if it comes suddenly.*

# GETTING THROUGH THE DAY

Another story from Professor LaGrand's book comes from Christine, whose husband, Jay, was murdered. About three weeks after Christine's husband was killed, she began dreaming about him. "I saw him as vivid as life," she explained. "He seemed happy and very healthy and peaceful." At first, he did not come close to Christine to kiss and hug her, however, explaining that "it was too soon" and she would need to be patient.

Jay told Christine that he knew how frustrated everyone was that his case had not been resolved. He gave her information about the crime scene and about those responsible for his murder. Jay told Christine who his actual killer was and who is accomplices were. Due to the lack of physical evidence, however, the police were unable to arrest these people.

"Yes," Christine commented, "some may say it's all in my mind, the grieving widow who wants to believe her husband talks to her. Well, I now do believe that Jay is around us and I now get those hugs and kisses when we meet in my dreams. It may be in my mind, and it may be hard to believe, but things that I have received from Jay's visits can never be explained to me, or anyone else...."

# Reflection

### Explanations Not Needed

*Those who demand scientific evidence*
*to prove that deceased loved ones*
*return to offer comfort, advice,*
*and sometimes other kinds of information*
*will have to go on waiting*
*because scientific information is not forthcoming.*
*Scientific knowledge has its limits*
*that some people are not willing to acknowledge.*
*The heart has its ways of knowing*
*that science will never be able to*
*evaluate, prove, or disprove.*

# THE HAPPY BIRTHDAY SONG

Mary's widowed mother died at the age of eight-three. She had given birth to two children, Mary and her brother, both born on September 8, two years apart. On the Roman Catholic liturgical calendar, September 8 is also the birthday of Mary, the mother of Jesus.

The September 8 following the death of Mary's mother, Mary had a Mass said for her mother in the parish church where she and her brother had been baptized, confirmed, and received their first holy Communion. This was also the church from which their mother had been buried.

Mary and her family and brother arrived a the church a bit early, and the organist was practicing. "Suddenly, the organist played the Happy Birthday song," Mary said. "We all looked at each other, quite surprised to hear this song being played in church. Of course, I was sure it was in honor of Our Lady's birthday. But when the organist played the same song again, we all had the same reaction. It is truly our feeling that this had to be our mother's message to my brother and me, 'Happy Birthday' once for my brother and once more for me."

There is no doubt in Mary's mind that this experience was "a loving sign from our mother."

## Reflection

**Birthday Glow**

*Did you ever stop to think*
*that God is glad that you were born?*
*We celebrate birthdays*
*with a cake and birthday candles,*
*with presents and the "Happy Birthday" song.*
*God celebrates our birthday, too,*
*and in good time*
*awaits our coming home.*

## "I SAW A CLOUD DRIFT SLOWLY BY"

Adrienne's father suffered a heart attack on May 13 and died on May 24. "The day he died," Adrienne said, "I had a doctor's appointment for my nine-month-old, and since we felt Dad was improving I thought it safe to miss that day's visit. My mother was with him when he quietly died about 5 P.M. She phoned my mother-in-law who lived nearby and asked her to come tell me."

When Adrienne's mother-in-law arrived, she was in her kitchen feeding the baby. The baby's high chair was near a window, and moments after she received the news Adrienne glanced out the window. "I saw a cloud drift slowly by," she said, "and it actually seemed to momentarily stop, and a voice said, 'A year from today you'll have a baby to take my place.' It was not exactly my father's voice, but it seemed to be him speaking through someone else."

Amazed that all this seemed so natural, Adrienne simply accepted it with no particular reaction. She didn't even comment about it to her mother-in-law. During the days that followed, she still could not bring herself to tell anyone. "But it served to bring me peace and strength," she explained, "during the days of the wake and funeral. At twenty-four, this was the first time I had experienced death so close to me, and this experience served to assure me that my father was all right. Heaven, an eternal afterlife, the communion of saints, all the things I had taken on faith I now knew to be irrefutably true."

Later that year, Adrienne conceived and, at the time, gave no thought to the voice from the cloud. In fact, she had not thought about it since May. The doctor told her the baby would be born in April, but the end of April came and still the baby had not been born. The doctor advised inducing labor. "For the first time in almost a year, I had a strong recollection of 'the cloud,' and I told my husband, 'No, we'll wait. This baby will be born sometime around the time Daddy died.'"

On May 13 a year later, a few minutes before midnight—the first anniversary almost to the minute of Adrienne's father's fatal heart attack—she gave birth to a baby boy. "We named him Theodore Paul," Adrienne said. "Theodore because we liked the nickname, Ted. Paul for the priest who had witnessed our marriage and had become a dear friend."

Adrienne and her husband had never read any books about the meanings of names, so they were surprised to learn later from several people that their new baby's name means "little gift from God." Adrienne found it noteworthy that no one had ever looked up the meaning of their first baby's name. As the days passed, however, Adrienne once again gave no further conscious thought to the "communication"—which she today considers miraculous—from her father.

Many years later, on the twentieth anniversary of the funeral and burial of Adrienne's father, she awakened with "a strong urge to go to Mass." As Adrienne debated with herself about this, the telephone rang with a call from Ted who was away at college. "He had been planning to come home that day but was delaying a day or two. He was very upset. A close friend had been diagnosed with a brain tumor and was to be operated on that day."

Adrienne decided right away to attend Mass and offer it for her son's friend. She would also ask her father for his prayers.

Later that day, Ted called. "When they operated there was no sign of the tumor which had been plainly visible in the x-ray. The boy was fine. There was no explanation."

## Reflection

**It's Amazing**

*Who knows the power people may have from God
once they pass over into eternity?
Benjamin Franklin said:
"Death is as necessary to the constitution
as sleep:
we shall rise refreshed
in the morning."*

*It's amazing, sometimes,*
*what we can do*
*when we're truly rested.*

# A BEDSIDE VISION

Gloria's younger brother, Jimmy, died at the age of thirty-one. "A few weeks after his death," Gloria said, "my Dad got up one morning and said that Jimmy had come to him and stood at the foot of his bed. He did not say anything, he just smiled as if to let him know he was okay. There was light all around him, and he looked about seventeen years of age. My dad said he was real, not a dream."

After her brother's death, Gloria would go to bed at night, as usual, and the minute she put her head on the pillow, she said, "someone or something would go around my bed pressing the mattress down....Then he would set on the edge of the bed. I know he was sitting because the mattress would go down as if someone was sitting on it. Then he would lay down beside me, and I could feel the motion and movement of the mattress next to me."

Gloria would lay in her bed completely still, terrified. "And then he would put his arm around my shoulder as if to comfort me. I know this, but I was still frightened. I would jump up out of bed and quickly turn on the lights to see who was there. Of course, the room was empty." This same experience happened night after night, Gloria said, "for a month or two."

When her brother died, Gloria took it very hard. "We were extremely close," she said, "and I missed him very much. I could not stop crying for him. He left a wife and two children. My sister-in-law decided to move to Florida with the children. I did not want her to go because she began drinking heavily when my brother died, and I was concerned for the children."

Each night, Gloria would go to bed and "cry all night," she said, and in the morning she would get up and go to work. "Every private moment during the day I would cry for him and his children. Then at night again the "comforting ghost"—which I now believe was my brother—would come again and do the same ritual every night. Of course, I did not find it comforting at the time. I was always scared."

Then one night Gloria went to bed and she thought she fell asleep. "My brother appeared at my bedside. He was alive, he was dimensional, like in a dream. There was light all around him. He appeared to be as my father had seen him, about seventeen years old. But unlike with my father, Jimmy spoke to me. He said that he did not want me to cry anymore. He said the name of a person and said that person was going to die, but that he would 'take care of them.' I didn't know what this meant. But he was so real, I know it was not a dream."

Gloria ran downstairs to tell her parents, but she could not remember the name of the person her brother had said was going to die. She tried to remember the name, but to no avail. "I kept thinking that maybe he was talking about my son. Jimmy was very close to my son because he felt bad that he had no father and felt that every child needs a father. He would come to my house every week to take him out and play with him."

Not long after Jimmy's appearance to Gloria, his widow—Gloria's sister-in-law—was killed in an auto accident. "My older brother, who already had five children, adopted the two young children, and they grew up in a wonderful, loving and caring home."

The day Gloria's sister-in-law died, her mother said, "That was the name you couldn't remember when Jimmy told you who was going to die."

I realized later than when Jimmy said he was going to 'take care of them' he was talking about his children."

# Reflection

### Alive and Caring

*Those who have died*
*continue to care deeply*
*for those they left behind.*
*Yet we think of them as*
*gone, gone, gone.*
*"Deader than a doornail,"*
*we say.*
*On the contrary,*
*they are more alive*
*than we can begin to imagine.*
*And they care for us deeply.*

# "SHE FLEW OUT THE OPEN WINDOW"

Diana's grandmother died at the age of ninety-five. "Although I knew she had lived a long life," Diana said, "it was still very painful to see her go. We had a very close relationship with each other. I grew up with the blessing of having her live with us throughout my childhood and into my adult life."

Diana believes that her grandmother loved all of her grandchildren, but Diana always felt like her grandmother's favorite. "I think the bond between us was so strong because she served, unplanned, as my mother's midwife when I was born at home."

When Diana's grandmother passed away, Diana was twenty-five years old and still living at home. Six months before her death, Diana's grandmother was no longer able to speak, then she became ill and was taken to the hospital where she quickly went into a coma.

One week after her grandmother's death, Diana had a dream.

"In my dream," she said, "I was walking out of my bedroom and looked into her bedroom which was right next to mine. And there was Grandma sitting on her bed with a big smile on her pretty face. Her cheeks were rosy, and there was a bright light glowing all around her. I ran as fast as I could and threw my arms around her, hugging her as tight as I could. Then I said, 'You're back—I can't believe you're really back. But how can this be true? You're dead!'"

Diana kissed her grandmother's cheek and told her how much she loved her and how much she missed her. "Then Grandma looked at me and said, 'I can't stay. I must return. I just wanted you to know that I'm fine and happy.'"

"Please don't leave me," Diana replied. "If you can't stay, then please take me with you."

"Where I am going," Diana's grandmother said, "you cannot go because it is not your time. But someday we will be together again."

"With that," Diana said, "she gave me a kiss and wrapped in light she flew out the open window. I looked out the window as she flew higher and higher until the heavens opened up, and she went in and all that remained in the sky was a beautiful white dove."

When Diana awoke, she wondered if all this had been a dream because it had seemed so real. "This experience brought me great comfort," she said. "I believe God allowed me to have this experience for a chance to say goodbye to Grandma."

# Reflection

### Eternal Life Is Now

*William Temple,*
*a seventeenth-century English author and statesman,*
*said:*
*"The life of faith does not earn eternal life;*
*it is eternal life.*

*And Christ is its vehicle."*
*We think that we must wait until after death*
*before we have eternal life.*
*On the contrary,*
*through loving intimacy with God*
*in this life*
*we already begin to share in*
*eternal life,*
*right now,*
*here and now.*
*Imagine that.*

# "She Never Abandoned Me"

Ruth's friend Elizabeth became a convert to the Roman Catholic faith at the age of seventy-five. Shortly after her reception into the church, on the eve of her confirmation, Elizabeth suffered a fractured knee while prying a two-year-old from an escalator. After her discharge from the hospital, Ruth stayed with her, and that short stay ended up being a stay of twenty-one years.

"During those twenty-one years," Ruth said, "the blindness which I had known was coming to me took on many complications. When I lost or misplaced an item, all I had to do was to ask Elizabeth and she would produce it. Usually she would say nothing, she just smiled."

Elizabeth eventually died, but, Ruth said, "she has never abandoned me. My blindness is total now, so I need her help more often than when she lived. All I have to do is to ask her to help me find whatever I've misplaced. Sometimes the item seems almost to come to my fingers. At other times, she gives me the inspiration as to its whereabouts. Rarely is there a delay in her response...."

Elizabeth was almost two generations Ruth's elder. "She prayed me through difficult years and once told a friend that she would live as long as I needed her. But since God called her at ninety-five-plus, he has given her the freedom to help me out. I recognize that her wise counsels are still coming to me, too. Though she is no longer living in her body, we have the communion of saints."

## Reflection

**We're All in This Together**

*The Christian doctrine*
*of the communion of saints*
*is simple, really.*
*All it says is that once you buy the farm*
*you still live on the farm.*
*All it says is*
*that those who have gone before us*
*are still with us.*
*All it says is that past generations*
*still count*
*and must be taken into account.*
*In other words,*
*we're all in this together.*
*All of us.*

# "Do All Things in Love"

Nora's husband died suddenly a few days before his fiftieth birthday. A few months later, Nora was in bed in the early morning. "My husband came to me," she reported. "I was greatly surprised and asked him what he was doing here."

Then, without giving her husband a chance to reply Nora asked, "Are you in heaven?" He replied, "No." "Are you in hell?" she asked again. Her husband said, "No." She asked, "Is the place where you are nice?" He answered, "No."

Nora then asked her husband if he had met anyone he knew in this life. "No," he replied.

"At that point," Nora continued, "I became aware that he wanted me to be silent. I stopped asking questions, and he said, 'You are to do all things in love.' After he said this, he left in the direction from which he had come without turning around. He appeared a perfect age with no signs of imperfections of any kind. I know that this was not a dream but a real visit from the spirit world."

Nora and her adult daughter both had the same dream. "Both of us saw my husband tending bar quietly at a location he owned at one time early in our marriage. I said, 'Hello' to him when I saw him, but he didn't acknowledge me, just kept on working. I shared this with my daughter and we were both amazed at having exactly the same dream."

## Reflection

### Living in Love

*Visions and appearances,*
*visions and appearances,*
*and the message remains the same.*
*It's remarkable,*
*is it not?*
*Holy happenings,*
*messages from saints*
*and loved ones,*
*and what they say boils down to*
*the same thing we already knew.*
*We are to do all things in love.*
*Remember.*

# ONE MORE HUG

In her excellent little book, *The Pummeled Heart*, journalist and author Antoinette Bosco wrote about the death of her son. "What was most important to me after my son Peter died was to know that he was with God and happy," she said, "and I prayed for signs so I could know. Peter had seen his death as embarking on a journey to take him 'home,' and I accepted that, but being a mother, I wanted to know that he had reached his destination."

Two months after Peter's death, on Pentecost Sunday, Antoinette had spent a large part of the day with relatives, with whom she talked about and prayed for Peter. "I prayed for the Holy Spirit to comfort me, but in a very specific way. I asked to receive just one more hug from my son. That may have sounded like a dumb request, but I've never hesitated to ask God for specific perks, and I've never complained if the answer was 'no.'"

That night, Antoinette went to bed at about eleven o'clock. As she lay in bed praying, she was, she said, "jolted by a loud bang against the wall behind my bed. I stayed put, eyes closed, thinking it was just a peculiar 'house noise.'"

A few minutes passed, and "the bang hit again," this time "like a forceful slap against the outside wall of the house. This time I opened my eyes, and I was startled by what I saw. I have a cathedral ceiling in my bedroom, and there, on the right side, where there is no possibility of outside light coming in through a window, was a glorious shower of light, like a myriad of flowing, shining bubbles.'"

Antoinette said that at that moment she was "enveloped with a presence, from above my head to past my feet. It was as if I were covered with the most comforting, benevolent blanket that could be imagined. I had never felt such completeness. I smiled and said, 'Thank you, Lord,' for I knew that God had answered my prayer and given me the joy of one last hug from my son."

Some will not take her seriously, Antoinette said, "believing that I have a wild imagination, emanating from wishful thinking. They are wrong. This was grace, God's gift of love to help me understand still more what I am to learn from my son's death."

## Reflection

**God Is...**

*God is love,*
*the Scriptures tell us,*
*God is love.*
*How feeble we are, however,*
*in our faith.*
*Secretly, we suspect that maybe God is*
*Something Else,*
*Something Scary*
*(booga-booga-booga!)*
*that is going to get us*
*good and hard.*
*But God is love,*
*the scriptures tell us,*
*and sometimes we know it*
*without a doubt,*
*with everything that is in us.*

## "I'M IN HEAVEN NOW"

Harry had no brothers or sisters, so when his aged parents needed hospital care and, later, needed to be placed in a nursing home, all the responsibility fell to him. Harry's mother was dying of liver cancer, so he visited her often. In early June, Harry's high school teaching responsibilities kept him from visiting for a few days, however.

Harry went to visit his mother. The staff at the nursing home told him his mother had died three days ago. "She's in the morgue," Harry was told. "I was in a state of total shock," he said.

Harry immediately called his cousin. "Of course she was upset," he said, "but she told me a wonderful story. No one knew that my mother had died because no one had been told, but my cousin told me that on June 6 her son, who is a police officer, said a prayer for my mother, who had prayed for him for years. She prayed that he would be able to pass high school Spanish, and she prayed…that he would pass the police test. My cousin's son told her that the day after my mother died, when he prayed for her he heard her voice very clearly say, 'You don't have to pray for me, I'm in heaven now.'

"This incident has sustained me for years and probably will until I meet my mom again in heaven," Harry commented.

# Reflection

### The Gift of This Life

*We wonder and worry*
*about those who reach the end of their lives*
*before us.*
*Are they okay?*
*This is natural, to be expected.*
*But let us not neglect the gift of this life.*
*Albert Camus,*
*the great mid-twentieth-century French novelist and philosopher,*
*said:*
*"If there is a sin against life,*
*it lies perhaps less in despairing of it*
*that in hoping for another*
*and evading the implacable grandeur*
*of the one we have."*
*Mais, oui!*

# "THIS TOO SHALL PASS"

Carol learned that her former boss, Gloria, had suffered a severe stroke and would probably die soon. September 11 was a particularly difficult day for Carol, and to find comfort she picked up a book of daily meditations for women. The theme of the meditation for that day was, "This too shall pass."

"This saying was a favorite of Gloria's," Carol said. "She even had a plaque with these words on it in her office." Thinking of these words, Carol said, "Gloria, you died today, didn't you. Please pray for me."

"I felt that she answered that everything would work out," Carol said. "The next day, I was told that Gloria had died the day before."

## Reflection

**All That Matters Is Love**

*We get so tied up in knots
sometimes
about our everyday responsibilities,
and everyday irritations and frustrations
don't help.
But one of the clearest messages
of our own mortality is that
in any situation where things
don't go the way we want them to,
this, too, shall pass.
This, too, shall pass,
and all that really matters is
our love for one another
and for God.*

## ENOUGH IS ENOUGH

Father Basil, a Franciscan friar, said that his mother died, and fifteen years later he was ordained a priest. "I don't remember exactly how many years later," he said, "but early in my priesthood one morning while celebrating Mass, at the Memento for the Dead, I heard my mother's voice saying, very happily, in Polish, "That's enough."

A woman once told Father Basil that during World War II she was washing clothes in her basement when she saw her son, who was in the military, all in flames. "She went upstairs and again he appeared to her all in flames. She asked, 'Son what are you doing here?'

"She learned that he had been killed in action. She came to me asking whether she was insane. I assured her she was not."

## Reflection

### Perplexity and Faith

*Now and then,*
*an experience of a deceased relative or friend*
*can be perplexing,*
*rather than a great inspiration or comfort.*
*Faith in a loving God*
*overcomes even perplexity.*
*Love is all.*

## "PUT ON THE BRAKE!"

Paul was the founder of two different professional football teams. Jude worked for Paul during Paul's last year as a coach and then for seventeen years after Paul became an owner and general manager. "Paul was a many-sided genius who devoted himself to the sport of football," Jude said. "He could have been a successful lawyer, physician, or business and industrial tycoon, but football was his chosen field."

Paul gave Jude personal attention from the first day Jude went to work for him. Paul taught Jude how to evaluate potential players. "Many times I had a chance to leave Paul and to go work for another team," Jude said, but after everything was considered I always stayed with Paul and his team."

In later years, Paul became sick and was no longer active in football, but he and Jude still talked regularly by letter and by telephone. "What a shock it was to me," Jude said, "when his son, Pete, told me I was being let go because I no longer fit into the future plans."

The next day, still in shock from being let go so unexpectedly, Jude called the owner of another professional football team and was immediately given another job. "When Paul found out," Jude said, "he called me and said that if he was still in charge this would not have happened. He was planning to involve me in pro scouting. He expressed concern for my family, my feelings and, most of all, he was concerned that our friendship would not be damaged. I assured him that would never happen."

During the two years before Paul's death, he and Jude became even greater friends, Paul sharing with Jude his private worries about family relationships. Paul belonged to the Episcopal Church, but was not a regular churchgoer. Still, Jude said, Paul had a deep spiritual side.

"I received notice of Paul's death while driving down the Interstate," Jude recalled. "A knot came into my throat, and I burst into tears. It was as if my father had died."

The funeral was open only to family, a few associates and former players, and Jude was unable to attend. The day of Paul's funeral, he attended Mass at a parish church and sensed Paul's presence expressing appreciation for the Mass and asking that other Masses be offered for him at a shrine where Paul and Jude had once attended Mass together following a practice for an important game.

"I had a dream," Jude said, "in which Paul came to me as I was sitting alone in a football stadium watching practice. He was a young man, like when he coached a professional team. He sat down beside me and commented on how lonely it must be to be on the road away from my family. Then he suggested I write a book about how he had taught me his method of scouting player personnel. 'Call it *A Scout is a Lonely Hunter*,' he said. I wrote the book in ten months, then turned it over to a friend of Paul's who plans to add some stories about Paul."

A couple of years later, Jude and his wife left home and drove toward a highway from a side street. The light was green, so they proceeded. "Suddenly," Jude said, "Paul's voice shouted 'Put on the brake!' I slammed on the brakes and stopped twenty feet from a runaway truck that had lost its brakes. This would have been sudden death. The truck ran off the road into a field and turned over. The driver was safe but slightly injured.

"I sat in total shock, and Paul's voice said, 'Be watchful and prayerful.' Paul has a spiritual contact with me, as I'm the person who prays for his repose. He knows he will soon be with his beloved first wife, Kate. Saving my life probably put him over the top and into perfect peace."

# Reflection

### Relax and Go to Bed

*Those who die*
*continue to have an interest*
*in what happens in this world,*
*especially in the lives of those*
*to whom they were close*
*in time and space.*
*Yet our fascination with the afterlife*
*can be misplaced.*
*Someone once asked John Wesley,*
*the eighteenth-century founder of the Methodist Church,*

*what he would do*
*if he knew that he would die that night.*
*Wesley replied*
*that he would eat his supper,*
*preach at the candlelight service,*
*say his prayers,*
*and go to bed.*
*To worry about death*
*is to worry about the ultimate*
*when it comes to things out of our control.*
*Say your prayers*
*and go to bed.*

# ASHES IN THE LIVING ROOM

Cathy's Japanese grandmother was a horror film aficionado, and as a child Cathy sometimes went along to see the latest scary movie. "I grew up thinking that Frankenstein's monster, the mummy, and the werewolf must have existed, even though I was told, 'It's just a movie!' I was too naive to figure out how they did it. Being the oldest of seven children raised in a typical Asian family in Hawaii, I was not encouraged to be an independent thinker."

Living for a time with Cathy and her family, Cathy's grandmother took her on bus rides, shopping, picnics, and to Japanese dancing school. Then, about the time Cathy started school her grandmother moved back to Japan. After that, her visits were infrequent and, while Cathy had pleasant memories of her grandmother she was "too busy doing my own thing" to get very close. "The last time I saw her," Cathy said, "I was a very sports-minded ninth grader who played a lot of tennis. My grandmother told my mother I was getting very vain because I was putting on makeup. My mother had to explain that I was just tan from the sun."

Soon after this, Cathy's grandmother died in Japan, and her father went to Japan for the funeral services. "He had her body

cremated and brought her ashes back to Hawaii for final inter-
ment," Cathy said.

Cathy's family lived in a two-bedroom, one bath house and,
she said, "I had the honor of sleeping in the living room by myself." The night her father brought her grandmother's ashes back
from Japan, he put them in the living room, and Cathy made "a
big fuss" over having to sleep in the same room. Her fear of the
unknown and having the ashes of a dead person in the same room
was so great that she could not go to sleep.

"Finally," Cathy said, "I had a 'dream' that wasn't a dream.
My grandmother appeared to me and asked me why I was so afraid
of her. Didn't I know that she loved me and would never do anything to hurt me? When that happened I remembered the love she
had for me, and I immediately went into a peaceful sleep. It has
been many years since this event, but I can still remember it. Love
never diminishes!"

## Reflection

### Believing Is Seeing

*Perhaps we say, over and over,*
*that we do believe in eternal life,*
*an eternal life which begins here*
*and finds its ultimate fulfillment*
*on the other side of natural death.*
*Still, when something happens to make it plain*
*that what we say we believe is, in fact, true,*
*we are startled and comforted.*
*Imagine that, what we say we believe is true!*
*At other times, people find themselves*
*believing almost in spite of themselves.*
*Take the great nineteenth-century French scientist,*
*Louis Pasteur, for example.*
*As his daughter lay dying, he said:*

*"I know only scientifically determined truth,*
*but I am going to believe*
*what I wish to believe,*
*what I cannot help but believe is*
*I expect to meet this dear child*
*in another world."*

# GOOD TO BE HOME

Author Patricia Livingston wrote in a magazine article that as she drove home from her mother's funeral, "a thousand thoughts and feelings filling my world." Midway through the fourteen-hour trip, Patricia realized that for the first time since she was thirteen years old she would not be calling to tell her mother she had made it home safely.

"She kept track of all my trips," Patricia wrote, "which was quite a feat since I was on the road for a living for ten years. We had a ritual. I would call no matter when it was and say, 'Hi, Mom. I made it home safely.' And she would say, 'Oh good, I bet it's good to be home.' And I would say, 'It really is. It is good to be home.'"

When Patricia drove in her driveway late that July evening, she was "stiff and sore and sad." As she carried her luggage into her room, she glanced at the telephone. "I felt the wrench of the summer," she wrote, "the terrible grimness of her slow death, the indignity, the pain, the struggle it took to do the simplest things: swallow, breathe, turn over. I was very glad that her anguish was over, but I could hardly stand it that I would not talk to her again."

Suddenly, Patricia heard a voice inside herself. "Not out loud. I don't know how to explain it, but it was her voice. It was as if she were saying, 'Now it's my turn. I am calling you. I made it home safely. It's good to be home.'

"I had an image of light coming on at the bottom of the attic steps," Patricia continued, "and of her calling up, 'Don't let the Devil steal your joy.'"

# Reflection

### Fear Is Not Necessary

*We are meant to find joy in life,*
*but so much of the time*
*we allow the cares and concerns of daily life*
*to steal our joy.*
*If those who have gone before us*
*have anything*
*they have pure joy.*
*Joy is what faith is supposed to bring us.*
*Yet how many so-called believers live lives*
*that are grimsville.*
*Faith means there is no need to be grim,*
*no need to fear anything,*
*especially God.*
*Joy.*

# "COME"

Sister Mary, a Roman Catholic nun, died after living with Multiple Sclerosis for thirty-eight of her sixty-eight years. Her friend, Sister Lucille, was at her side.

"We had (and still have) a most wonderful, loving relationship," Sister Lucille said. "She was twenty-three years older than I and my youth helped her through many trying times."

Sister Lucille accompanied Sister Mary Patricia on many outings, and when she was no longer able to get in a van or car, Sister Lucille wheeled her around in their religious community's home for sick and elderly nuns. When she was able to visit—usually on weekends and holidays—Sister Lucille worked along with the nursing staff to care for Sister Mary.

"We also had a very spiritual side to our friendship," Sister

Lucille said. "We prayed together, we sang liturgical music together, we read Scripture. You name it, we did it all. When Mary died I felt as though half of me went with her and the other half is waiting to join her."

There is, however, another person in this story. "Her name was Sister Francis," Sister Lucille said. "She was a peer of Mary's in the community. She died very suddenly of a heart attack. The three of us had become a trinity-of-sorts in the summer years before when I first began my friendship with Mary. What a team!"

During the last two months of her life, Sister Mary suffered a great deal. Sister Lucille was with her as much as she could be. Sister Lucille described the day Sister Mary died, as "the most loving day in my life thus far. Everything I did for and with Mary that day was so centered in love."

Sister Lucille had often spoken with Sister Mary about looking for her deceased mother and father. Since Sister Francis' death, Sister Mary had often spoken of a boat coming for her to meet Jesus, so that day Sister Lucille also spoke about Sister Francis coming for her in the small boat.

"As she was expiring," Sister Lucille said, "I beheld the most beautiful face of a child on my friend's face. When her chest had stopped moving and her eyes had become fixed in an open position, I called for the nurses. I stepped out of the room to let the nurses tend to Mary's dead body. Then I went right back in.

"As I stood next to her bed I was right next to the two nurses. I tried looking towards Mary's now lifeless face. As I did this, my eyes were drawn to the space between the wall and the nurses. There was Francis. I could see her trim frame; I could see through her. She had on a flowered blouse and a white skirt. I had one thought as she stood there: What will she do? Will she gesture to Mary to go with her? Then the word 'COME' went all through my being. As soon as I sensed that word, Francis disappeared.

"She never moved during the entire vision. She just looked at Mary with her peace-filled eyes (as she always did when she was alive), and her whole being said 'COME'." Then Mary exhaled one final breath, and I felt, I knew, her spirit had gone with Francis."

Sister Lucille added that she feels compelled to tell this story to whoever will listen. "It has been such a consolation to me during my grieving to know that Francis came for Mary. And that vision was pure gift. I've never ever had an experience like that."

But this was not the end of the story. The following summer, Sister Lucille made a retreat, still grieving for Sister Mary. One day, sitting in the chapel, she felt quite empty but, at the same time, strangely peaceful. "The room was bright and airy," she said, "and there was no one else with me. I was missing Mary very much. As I sat on this comfy chair, I felt a gentle breeze on my left hand—just my hand. Then, out of nowhere I had the thought, 'Mary, reveal yourself to me.' At that moment the breeze came back again and traveled along my arm and went across my left cheek. In life, I had often held Mary's left hand and rubbed that arm and planted a kiss on her left cheek when she was hurting.

"Again I felt a deep consolation knowing Mary was still close to me. I just can't see her with my earthly eyes. I must look for her with the eyes of my soul."

# Reflection

### Friendship Is a Little Sacrament

*There is, perhaps, no gift in this life greater*
*than friendship,*
*especially a friendship that brings you closer to God.*
*"Faithful friends*
*are a sturdy shelter,"*
*says the Book of Sirach:*
*"whoever finds one has found*
*a treasure.*
*Faithful friends are beyond price;*
*no amount can balance their worth.*
*Faithful friends are life-saving medicine;*
*and those who fear the Lord*
*will find them" (6:14-16).*

*Each true friend we find is*
*a visible sign of an invisible reality—*
*a visible sign of our Ultimate Friend, our loving God.*
*Claude de la Colombière, a seventeenth-century mystic,*
*addressed a prayer about friendship to Jesus,*
*his Ultimate Friend:*
*"O Jesus, You are my true Friend, my only Friend.*
*You take part in all my misfortunes;*
*You take them upon Yourself;*
*You know how to change them into blessings.*
*You listen to me with greater kindness*
*when I relate my troubles to You,*
*and You always have balm*
*to pour on my wounds.*
*I find You at all times;*
*I find You everywhere;*
*You never go away;*
*If I have to change my dwelling,*
*I find You wherever I go."*

# SIGNS OF LOVE

The first time Helen visited the cemetery, after the death of her father, she was accompanied by one of her brothers and a sister. "We were commenting about the plants and flowers in front of some of the tombstones," she said. "We discussed the care they would need and how often they were ruined when mowing was done. We said that it was a shame we didn't adorn Dad's grave site, as he loved flowers—the outdoors, all of nature—so much."

Then Helen noticed a small orange flower with a yellow center, all by itself, almost touching her father's tombstone. "It was the same wild flower that blooms in a field behind my house," she said. "The only other time I saw one anywhere else was on a walk with my Dad near his home the year before he died."

Helen looked more closely. There were no other wild flowers of any kind anywhere nearby. "I got goosebumps and chills," she said. "It was a certain sign to me of my father's presence with God. Although I already believed he was there, this was a confirmation. Whenever I think about this, I get a renewed feeling that he is continuing to love and help me from his heavenly home."

# Reflection

### Praising Fathers

*Fathers sometimes do not get as much appreciation*
*as they deserve.*
*Fathers, being men, sometimes get*
*a "bad rap" for simply being a part of their culture*
*and their time,*
*for following the rules they found in place*
*when they got there.*
*Many fathers do their best,*
*only to discover that their best wasn't good enough*
*for a society experiencing growing pains*
*in its attitudes towards women.*
*Mothers get a heap of appreciation,*
*hearts and flowers each Mother's Day.*
*Father's Day isn't as big a production.*
*Even the metaphor of God as our Father*
*is battered and bruised these days.*
*Maybe it's time to rehabilitate fatherhood,*
*and we can do no better than to keep in mind*
*the fathering image Gerard Manley Hopkins used*
*in one of his most famous poems, "Pied Beauty."*
*Thus:*
*"Glory be to God for dappled things—*
*For skies of couple-colour as a brindled cow;*
*For rose-moles all in stipple upon trout that swim;*
*And all trades, their gear and tackle trim.*

*All things counter, original, spare, strange;*
*Whatever is fickle, freckled (who knows how?)*
*With swift, slow; sweet, sour; adazzle, dim;*
*He fathers-forth whose beauty is past change;*
*Praise Him!"*
*This is what fathers are meant to do,*
*"father-forth" in their families*
*and in the world.*
*Even fathers who are not great fathers,*
*but good enough fathers,*
*deserve more praise than they sometimes get.*

# A DEEP SENSE OF WELL-BEING

After the death of their father, Laura and her mother and brothers were spiritually and emotionally devastated. "Our life as we knew it had crashed around us as a house when the central beam is removed," she said.

Laura said that she lost her will to live. "Subconsciously, I waited for my father to return so that the shattered pieces of our lives would be restored to their original state."

Then one night, Laura had a dream about her father. "I felt joy, love, and a deep sense of well-being in his presence," she said. "His message was clear. My father said that he wanted very much to be with us, implying that he was someplace else. I experienced great sadness over his separation from us and his great love and concern for each one of us."

When Laura awoke, her mood had shifted dramatically. "I was deeply comforted by the fact that although my father cannot 'be' with us, he wants to be with us and loves us greatly. This thought gave me great comfort, courage, and strength each time I thought of it. It helped me to go on with my life."

# Reflection

## Good Fathers

*Every coin has two sides, of course,*
*including the coin marked "fatherhood."*
*A father's gesture from eternity*
*is not to mysteriously go back*
*to his earthly job*
*and cause checks for large amounts of money*
*to arrive in the mail of the family*
*he left behind.*
*No, his gesture is to communicate his love*
*in words.*
*Many fathers think their main task in life*
*is to "bring home the bacon,"*
*and "keep their nose to the grindstone."*
*There is much truth here.*
*Work is an important way*
*that fathers, as well as mothers, love their family.*
*But that's not the whole tamale.*
*"It is easier for a father to have children,"*
*said Blessed Pope John XXIII,*
*"than for children to have a real father."*
*It is the task of a good father to simply*
*be there*
*with his children*
*as often as possible.*
*Years ago, when Paul Tsongas was a U. S. Senator*
*from Massachusetts,*
*he decided to not seek a second term*
*so he could spend more time with his wife and children.*
*He told the press:*
*"No man on his deathbed ever said,*
*'I wish I had spent more time at the office.'"*

# PURE JOY

When Marie was twelve years old, her eighteen-year-old brother was killed while riding his bike by a hit-and-run drunk driver. "Gary was...my best friend and confidante," Marie recalled. "He was very gifted in many areas, including drama, art, singing, science and math, and he had a great love of nature. Gary would often wake me up in the middle of the night to go on hikes, just to observe the forest in the beauty of Minnesotan winters. He would often write poetry after such treks, which I now have and still read from time to time."

Marie was shattered and inconsolable when Gary was killed. Her parents withdrew into their grief and found it difficult to speak of him at all. Marie begged to move into Gary's room, and her parents agreed. This seemed to help her work through some of her grief, but even five years later she dreamed frequently of Gary. In her dreams, she would try to reach him by running to hug him, overjoyed that he was still alive. But in each dream when she tried to put her arms around Gary he would disappear, and she would wake up in tears.

"Finally," Marie said, "about ten years after Gary's death, I had a dream in which I saw him in our driveway sitting on the bike that he'd been riding when he was killed. The sun was shining in my dream, and the air was warm outside. I again ran to him, and this time I actually felt the solidity of his body. The emotion of pure joy coursed through me, and then Gary said, 'There, now you can move on, Marie. I am happy, I am here with you.'"

Waking up, Marie felt deeply peaceful. "I have never had any more dreams of Gary associated with shattering loss and deep, unrequited grief," she said. "I thought then, as I do now, that he was really there, and his purpose was to help me to resolve years of inconsolable pain from the tragedy of his sudden death."

# Reflection

### Death Isn't the Worst Thing

*There are many humorous euphemisms*
*for dying.*
*She "kicked the bucket," we say,*
*or he "bought the farm."*
*A movie cowboy who dies*
*went to "that big roundup in the sky."*
*Someone who dies "croaked," we say.*
*"She's pushing up daisies,"*
*and "he's six feet down."*
*There is a time and a place for such humor,*
*certainly not at a time of bereavement*
*with those close to the person who died.*
*Still, to use such humor*
*is to cultivate a healthy attitude towards death.*
*After all, such humor says,*
*death is not the worst thing*
*that can happen to a person.*
*Repeatedly, stories of encounters*
*with deceased relatives or friends*
*suggest that in the grand scheme of things*
*death is small potatoes.*

# TRANSPORTED INTO A GARDEN

Marian grew up during the Great Depression of the 1930s, living with her parents, her maternal grandmother, and an older sister who was mentally handicapped. Her mother and grandmother were "deeply devout Catholics," while her Irish father "drank when the coins jingled in his pockets."

Many years later, her grandmother and mother long gone, Marie found it necessary to place her father—now in poor health—and her sister in institutions where they could receive the care they required. Eight years later, her father had a stroke and died the next day. Marie's sister was "so lost as she tried to figure out why he left us."

The two days following the death of her father Marie was filled with sorrow as, alone, she went about the tasks of preparing for the burial. "The night before the funeral," she said, "I awoke about 2 A.M. filled with a terrible loneliness. Suddenly, I felt myself being transported into a garden at twilight or early dawn. There were shadowy trees, sounds of birds softly calling, the sweet perfume smells of a garden. At a distance I saw a figure. It seemed to be reclining. I watched with no fear at all. The figure beckoned to me to approach, which I did with no fear or hesitation. The figure drew me down into an embrace, where we remained for some time. I felt such a sense of peace and joy. Together we arose, each walking on a different path. I left the way I had entered the garden, through a heavily leafed gateway. I fell asleep then with the certain feeling that this was not a dream."

The next few days were untroubled, Marie said. "Now I look back and think that it had to be a dream. But I am convinced that it was Jesus in the garden. He knew I was alone...."

# Reflection

**Victory Over Fear**

*Our peace of mind
and sense of personal security
are so fragile.
Almost anything, it seems,
can cause us to feel anxious and afraid.*

*In the early part of the twentieth century,*
*a Russian writer named Nikolai Berdyaev*
*said that fear is never a good counselor*
*and that victory over fear is*
*our first spiritual duty.*
*This is what we learn*
*from those who "return"*
*from the eternal realm*
*to comfort us.*
*Don't be anxious or afraid, they say.*
*Everything is fine, go on living.*

# THE LAUGHING DRUNKEN FOOL

Mary Anne's maternal grandmother fell and broke her hip. Since she lived on the fourth floor of a walk-up apartment building, she moved to a nursing home to recuperate. A few weeks later, Mary Anne's father died suddenly. "Our family decided not to tell Grandma because we didn't want to trouble her," Mary Anne said. "She wouldn't be able to come to the funeral. No one told her, and there was no way she could have found out that my father was gone."

The day after Mary Anne's father died, her aunt went to see Mary Anne's grandmother. "When she saw my aunt," Mary Anne said, "she said to her, 'Don't you have something to tell me?' My aunt replied, 'What are you going on about, Mother?' Grannie said, 'You can't fool me. He was here.' My aunt said, 'Who was here?' 'The laughing drunken fool, Eddie, was here!' she said. 'I couldn't get a word out of him because all he did was keep laughing at me.' 'Why didn't you tell me about what happened to Mary [Mary Anne's mother] and who she had in a box?' Grannie asked. 'I know all about it!'"

Mary Anne's aunt was shocked that "Grannie" knew what had happened, but she thought that "Grannie" was imagining things when it came to Mary Anne's father being there. "He was a great laugher," Mary Anne explained, "and always fond of alcohol."

The following day, Mary Anne's aunt returned to visit "Grannie" again, only to learn that "he was back again," and still laughing. This time he came eating hot dogs, his favorite food, and still "drunk as a skunk."

The day after her father died, Mary Anne's friend, Angy—one of her father's favorite people—called to tell her that she had a strange dream. Mary Anne's father was sitting in a green field, and all he did was laugh. He never spoke. Mary Anne then told Angy about her father's death, which took Angy completely by surprise.

Two weeks after her father's death, Mary Anne visited with her neighbor, Juanita, who asked Mary Anne what was wrong with her father. Juanita obviously did not know that he had died, so Mary Anne told her. "No, no, no," Juanita insisted, "last week he was standing on the steps laughing at me." Mary Anne said, "I swear, he's been dead for two weeks." Juanita's face went pale as she told Mary Anne that she saw her father, she was absolutely positive.

Meanwhile, Mary Anne's grandmother was never able to leave the nursing home. A few weeks after Mary Anne's father died, her grandmother told her that her long-dead husband and two of her children who had died visited her earlier that day. Mary Anne asked what they wanted. Her grandmother replied that they wanted her to go with them.

On New Year's Eve, Mary Anne invited friends for her traditional New Year's Eve party. "All my friends came over," she said, "and we had a great party." Mary Anne didn't make it to bed until 5:00 A.M. "I looked at the clock as I got into bed, so I'm positive that it was 5:00 A.M."

Mary Anne fell asleep, then she felt someone kiss her on the cheek. "I thought it was my roommate, John, acting stupid (something he did quite often) so I got up and looked at the clock. It was 7:00 A.M."

Looking in all the other rooms, however, Mary Anne found

no one else. She knew someone had kissed her, however. "To this day, I can still feel this kiss." Giving up the search, she returned to bed.

At 7:30, however, Mary Anne's phone rang. It was her mother calling to tell her that her grandmother had died at 7:00 A.M. Mary Anne immediately thought, "Now I know who kissed me."

# Reflection

### The Mystery of Love

*We use the word "love"*
*with such nonchalance*
*when what we're talking about*
*is an overwhelming mystery.*
*After all, "God is love."*
*Love is what brings us together and makes us complete.*
*"Only love can bring individual beings*
*to their perfect completion as individuals,"*
*wrote Teilhard de Chardin,*
*"because only love takes possession of them*
*and unites them*
*by what lies deepest within them."*
*Even after death,*
*love between people*
*continues to be real.*

# THE PROMISE

Michiko, a devout Catholic, came in to clean Clay's house on Monday, her regular day. As it happened, this was a few days following the sudden death and funeral of Clay's wife, Myra. Still saddened, Michiko gathered herself together and went about her cleaning duties.

Entering Clay and Myra's bedroom on the second floor,

Michiko found Myra lying on the bed. Startled and frightened, Michiko asked, "What are you doing here? You're dead!"

Myra replied, "Yes, I know. I've come back to tell you that now that I'm gone Clay is going to need your help more than ever. I'm asking you to stay on as long as he needs you."

Michiko agreed to do this, and Myra then vanished. In a state of shock, Michiko went back downstairs where Myra's visiting mother noticed how pale Michiko's face was and insisted that she go home and rest.

Ten years later, Clay's children were all grown and on their own, and he had no further need for Michiko to come in weekly to clean the house. Not having the heart to break this news to a woman who had become a dear friend—believing she might still need the work—he wrote Michiko a letter of gratitude and thanks and enclosed a check for severance pay.

Later, Michiko called and talked to Clay's secretary, explaining that she was relieved to get his letter. She had wanted to stop coming in to clean for a year now but she had felt that she must have some sign that Clay no longer needed her. She then told the secretary the story of her encounter with Myra after her death. "Now I have kept my promise to Myra," Michiko said.

# Reflection

### Listening to Your Heart

*Poet Robert Frost wrote about having*
*"promises to keep."*
*Love and faithfulness,*
*keeping promises,*
*are the concerns of those who love,*
*whether they are in this world or the next.*
*We may investigate this faithful love*
*that is beyond space and time*
*and in space and time*
*as it is reflected in the stories in this book.*

*But there comes a point*
*where the intellect must fall silent,*
*and gladly.*
*For kept promises need no justification or explanation.*
*They have meaning in themselves.*
*In the seventeenth-century words of Blaise Pascal,*
*"It is the heart which experiences God*
*and not the reason."*

# A LOCKSMITH
# KEEPS ON WORKING

Mary, a Catholic nun, said that her experience with deceased persons "is couched in a firm belief in the communion of saints, that death is 'simply' the passage experienced into the next phase of eternal life."

Mary said that the husband of a dear friend was a locksmith. "On my many travels, I ask Mr. Martin to help me keep track of my keys, especially the car keys. At points of near mishap he seems pretty tangibly present."

## Reflection

**A Little Less Skepticism**

*Maybe our friends and relatives*
*who are in eternity*
*would seem closer to us than they do*
*if we were less skeptical*
*about their continued existence.*
*For "those who do the will of God*
*live forever" (1 John 2:17).*

# "IT'S ME, ROBERT"

Brother Warren belongs to a Catholic community of Brothers dedicated to healing ministries. His particular ministry is that of a Patient Representative in one of his community's hospitals. One autumn, Brother Warren visited a young man age 35 named Robert, who was very ill with pneumonia.

"As we talked," Brother Warren said, "he told me that he had not been feeling well for a long time and recently found out that he had AIDS. I visited him daily, and he revealed a great deal of his life history."

Each time Brother Warren visited, Robert asked him to help him do some "centering prayer." Time passed, and Robert became progressively worse. Then one evening, he went into respiratory distress and was transferred to the Intensive Care Unit where he was put on a respirator to help him breathe.

"Two or three times a day," Brother Warren recalled, "I held Robert's hand, helped him to 'center,' and prayed with him. Each time we finished praying, he would write on a sheet of paper (he could not talk because of the respirator) how consoling and helpful our prayer sessions were to him."

Robert also said to Brother Warren that he hoped he would be with him when God called him to eternal life. "I said I would be with him when God called," Brother Warren said. "Unfortunately, I had to go out of town for a meeting and told him I would be back to see him in a week. He wrote on his pad of paper that he would miss me and would look forward to my return. He seemed to be progressing somewhat, so I told him that by the time I returned he would probably be off the ventilator and back to a regular room."

When Brother Warren returned a week later, he learned that Robert had died four days earlier. "I was devastated," he said, "particularly since I promised to be with him during his last days."

About a month later, Brother Warren went away for a private retreat. "One evening as I sat in a chair in my room reading the Scriptures, I suddenly felt Robert's presence. Although I did not literally 'see' or 'hear' him, his 'presence' sat on the edge of the bed which was next to the chair I was sitting in. He said to me, 'It's me, Robert. Why have you been feeling so guilty about not being with me when I died? You *were* there—not in body, but in spirit. You were very much with me. Please tell my mom and dad that I am very, very happy—the happiest I have ever been and that I am at peace.' Suddenly, Robert's presence was gone."

Brother Warren commented: "I have absolutely no doubt that this episode was not a product of my imagination, but a reality more real than anything I have physically seen, touched, or felt."

## Reflection

### Scientific Proof for Love?

*Our scientific culture does us a disservice*
*when it leads us to believe*
*that reality is limited*
*to what our physical senses can perceive.*
*Prove to me scientifically, for example,*
*that you love someone.*
*Prove to me, scientifically,*
*that love exists.*
*Show me a relationship between two people*
*under a microscope.*
*It can't be done,*
*yet who would deny that love is real?*

# WHERE THE FUN IS

Paul explained that his cousin, Jack, died of cancer. "He was a committed Catholic, had raised a family, received holy Communion daily, had a wonderful sense of humor, and as a lawyer was widely respected as fair and honest, which is quite a distinction these days."

Jack's cancer lingered for six months, which included chemotherapy treatments. "I had an opportunity to visit him about six weeks before he died," Paul recalled.

On the day of Jack's death, Paul was weeding in his garden at his summer cottage. "I remember the details very clearly," Paul said. "Jack spoke to me undeniably with these words: 'Paul, it's great fun here.' So clear was his voice, and so sure was I that this was my cousin that I actually got up off my knees and looked around for Jack in the direction of the voice. At that point, I was utterly convinced Jack had died, although it took three days for the family to contact me about his death. I subsequently learned that his speaking to me coincided closely with the day and time of his death."

Later, when Paul told his story to Jack's family it was met with skepticism. "One member of the family, his sister, said to me, 'Jack would never have talked like that.' I assumed she felt Jack was talking about heaven in an irreverent way. But the amusing thing is that I felt and still feel that that is exactly how Jack would talk about the kingdom of heaven."

# Reflection

### Heaven for the Fun of It

*Enough, already, with images of heaven*
*filled with be-winged beings*
*plucking on harps.*
*Why shouldn't heaven be fun?*
*In heaven, one may expect to meet*
*Laurel and Hardy.*
*Stan will doff his derby hat,*
*scratch his unkempt head of hair,*
*and do his funny "cry."*
*Ollie will do his famous tie twiddle,*
*and everyone will laugh.*
*Heaven will be fun.*

# REACHING OUT

Mary Ellen thinks of herself as a non-dreamer, except that scientists say we all dream but not everyone remembers their dreams. Yet she had a most remarkable dream.

"My mother died suddenly," Mary Ellen said. "It was on the same day I taught school for the first time after twenty years of being a homemaker. It was a substitute teaching assignment, and my mother was very excited to see me return to the classroom. She and I were very close friends, as well as mother and daughter."

Mary Ellen took her mother's death very hard. Two weeks after the funeral, she was depressed and physically exhausted. "I had foolishly accepted an assignment to substitute teach in a sixth grade class for two consecutive days. The night before the assignment I knew I was totally incapable of fulfilling it."

Under the circumstances, Mary Ellen decided to call in sick the next morning. "I am a sincerely responsible person, so to renege on this commitment was an indication of how seriously despondent I felt that tonight," she said. "I knew I could not manage the duties of this job."

Getting into bed, Mary Ellen fell asleep immediately, and during the night she dreamed.

"My mother was visiting me and doing some of the family laundry in the basement of my old house. The cellar steps are steep, and I had always told my mother to call one of my five children to carry the heavy laundry baskets for her. Usually she ignored his and did it herself. In the dream, she carried a basket of clean laundry up the cellar steps and entered my kitchen with it in her arms.

"I met her and jokingly reprimanded her by remarking, 'Gee, Mom, if you could balance another basket on top of your head, you'd be able to bring up two loads of laundry at one time!' She put the basket on the floor and reached out with a smile and embraced me. I felt her presence so powerfully at that moment."

Mary Ellen sat bolt upright in bed, fully awake. "I saw my room filled with a receding glow of light. Normally my room is in total darkness, and seeing the furniture is almost impossible. That night I could easily see my husband lying next to me and all the areas of the bedroom were visible for five to ten seconds. I could feel the presence of love, and I was completely unafraid. I felt very happy."

Lying down again, Mary Ellen felt asleep in great peace. "My mother had been with me. I knew that with every fibre of my being."

When she awoke the next morning, Mary Ellen was full of energy and confident of her ability to go into the classroom and do her job well. "I did not call in sick," she said. "Instead, I had a very rewarding day as a substitute teacher....

"This experience was a gift from God and my mother. To both, I am very grateful."

# Reflection

### Be Open Minded

*Those who are certain that*
*"when you're dead you're dead"*
*can't really be so certain.*
*Father Agnellus Andrew, a Franciscan priest,*
*was the British Broadcasting Corporation's*
*adviser on Roman Catholic affairs.*
*A producer planning programs on Catholicism*
*wrote Father Andrew a letter*
*asking how he might learn*
*the official Roman Catholic view of heaven and hell.*
*Father Andrew replied with a memo*
*that contained just one word:*
*"Die."*
*No one can be 100 percent positive of anything*
*about what happens after death*
*until they die.*
*Until then, even skeptics*
*do well to be open minded.*

# A SENSE OF HUMOR

Father Matt, a Franciscan, was killed by a drunk driver who ran a red light. Father Matt was only thirty-two years old and was on his way to a hospital to visit a sick person. This tragedy was a terrible blow to Father Matt's fellow Franciscans, said Brother Robert, who was a good friend of Father Matt. "It was a great shock to lose him so soon and so tragically," Brother Robert said.

The funeral Mass was celebrated in Fresno, California, where Father Matt had been killed, with burial following at the Franciscan novitiate in Santa Ynez. "That day was overcast and gray, threatening rain," Brother Robert recalled.

Near the end of the Mass, a ray of sun suddenly broke through, and the provincial, Father Gerald, commented on how Matt had arranged for some sun. "However," Brother Robert said, "when we left the chapel to drive in procession to the cemetery, it started to pour on us! The entire committal took place in the rain. Matt was always known for his sense of humor and his dislike of anything that sounded overly pious, so I said to one of my fellow friars that this was just like Matt, to rain on us, especially after the provincial's remark."

After the burial, the group moved to the nearby dining room for a small reception. "I had hung back," Brother Robert said, "and so came after everyone had already gone in. The clouds had begun to break up, and before going in I turned around to look back toward the cemetery. I was surprised to see a double rainbow, which ended right at the cemetery. It was very beautiful."

At that moment, Brother Robert felt Father Matt's presence, and he felt certain that he was still with his fellow Franciscans and had laughed with us when we got soaked. "I can't describe it beyond saying that it just seemed natural from that moment not to mourn Matt, but to remember him fondly and be glad that he had been with us and is still with us."

# Reflection

### Ordinary Comforts

*There is great comfort
in the natural events of everyday life,
especially when they happen
on extraordinary days.
Or perhaps it's the other way around.
Perhaps the ordinary events
are not ordinary at all,
and it takes an extraordinary event
to make us see how extraordinary
ordinary events always are.
A rainbow on an ordinary day
is just a beautiful rainbow.
But when the day isn't ordinary
we see that an ordinary rainbow is a revelation
and ordinary rain showers are messages
from God.
Always.*

# SOMEONE TO WATCH OVER ME

Shannon's father died of cancer when she was less than a year old. "I grew up knowing about him and his side of the family," she said, "but not him."

Many years later, Shannon helped staff a book store display for a conference. There wasn't time for her to attend any of the workshops except the one right next door to where the book display was set up. "The workshop was on inner healing," Shannon recalled, "which I usually avoided! I listened to the first part of the presentation, then after a short break the presenters began to lead the participants through a prayer of inner healing. I remember hearing them pray for people who had lost a parent, and I never heard another word."

Instead, Shannon found herself standing in a doorway, looking into a room where a man lay on a bed. "The blankets covered all but his face and arms. Between one arm and his body, there was a baby wrapped in a blanket. As I looked into the room, I felt someone behind me with a hand on my shoulder. I never looked around, but I knew it was Jesus and that the man on the bed was my father. It was a very peaceful scene, and I felt oddly comforted."

Some weeks later, Shannon told her mother about this experience. Her mother was quiet for a long time. "Your father used to do that," she finally said, and she told Shannon about the days when her father was very sick. "She would feed and change me, then bundle me up for a nap with my daddy. She'd never told me that part of the story, but I am sure that my skin remembered it somehow. This is a 'memory' that has given me comfort ever since then."

# Reflection

### A Parent's Love

*To know the love of a parent*
*is one of the most basic yearnings*
*of the human heart.*
*Sometimes this love can come to us*
*even across the apparent barriers*
*between dusty time*
*and golden eternity.*
*Sometimes this love can come to us*
*even when we don't ask for*
*or expect it.*
*The love of a parent*
*one never knew*
*is just as real and just as reliable*
*as the love of a parent*
*known for a lifetime.*

## "DAD WAS THERE"

In his book *Father and Son: Time Lost, Love Recovered*, Edward C. Sellner, a professor of theology, tells of a remarkable experience he had while visiting England, soon after the death of his father. After a pleasant evening in London, Sellner returned to his room. He wanted to pray in thanksgiving for all he had received on his journey and for a safe flight back to the United States.

"I turned out the overhead light and sat at the desk facing the full mirror. Then I lit a candle in front of the small icon of Jesus that I had carried along with me on my travels. I don't know how long I sat there staring into the flickering flame."

Suddenly as he prayed, it seemed to Edward Sellner that his father, dead for more than a month now, was with him. "It was as if the room filled with his presence, a presence almost palpable, as vivid and as real as if he had just physically entered the room, spoken to me, or touched my shoulder. This sense of his presence, initially so intense, frightened me."

Then Edward Sellner looked into the mirror in front of him: "I saw Dad's face; in the darkness I saw the reflection of an older face, as I remembered his, touched with sorrow, and yet strangely illuminated by the candlelight. The face in the mirror at first seemed to frown, "and then, as I continued to stare transfixed, [it] smiled reassuringly."

The entire experience lasted but a minute or two, "but it was as if I had entered some sort of timeless state. Dad was there, I could see him frowning and then smiling at me, and then he was gone. The intensity of the experience, however, no matter how long it actually lasted, left its imprint." He felt both afraid and awed.

Reflecting further on what had happened, Edward Sellner realized that the face in the mirror had been his own. And yet, it was *not* his. "It was Dad's." The smile he had seen on his father's face was the same smile he had seen when his father was alive; "the smile on his face when he held my own two sons in his arms; the smile I had seen that last visit before his stroke."

The experience of the face in the mirror reminded Edward Sellner that his father, "though dead, was very much alive. He not only lived somewhere in the spiritual realm, where souls wait for the resurrection, but in me, in my depth, in my heart."

# Reflection

### Love Is What Matters

*Those who have passed on*
*into the spiritual realm,*
*into a mysterious eternity,*
*seem to choose various ways to "return"*
*if they do "return."*
*Dreams,*
*actual physical presence*
*...a reflection in a mirror.*
*Does it really matter?*
*Probably not.*
*Those who "return"*
*seem matter-of-fact about being pragmatic.*
*Whatever works.*
*All that matters is the presence*
*of love.*
*For love is eternal.*

# "SEND ME A SIGN"

Ann thinks of herself as an educated person. She has a master's degree in political science and is halfway through the course work for a master's degree in theology. She does not think of herself as one inclined to believe in bizarre or extraordinary experiences related to "the beyond." But, she said, she could not deny her own experiences, all three of which involve her late father. "He was, by everyone's account, a saint as well as a magnificent Catholic and a great scholar."

When Ann was nineteen, her father and mother were killed in an auto accident. "There was enormous comfort in the fact that they were together," Ann said, "yet I still wanted assurance that they were okay. I was not irrational with grief, not doubtful at all that they were in heaven…I just wanted a sign, and I asked them for one. 'If you're okay,' I asked them as I left our house for their funeral, 'please let me see an incongruously red flower.'

Ann lived in Florida, and flowers—including red ones—were abundant that June afternoon, but Ann was confident that her parents would know what she meant. Arriving at the church, Ann found it filled with nothing but white flowers. "Believe me, I looked."

After the funeral, Ann and her relatives and friends returned home. On the table in the dining room was a huge bouquet of snowy white flowers someone had brought from the church. "In the midst of dozens of white blossoms was one bright red carnation," Ann recalled. "I had not told anyone of my request, and I suppose it could have been an accident, but it still seems strange to me to see one red flower among three dozen white ones, specifically sent for a funeral. At the time, I simply *knew* the flower was from them."

For three years prior to his death, Ann's father had tried many times to help her open an antique perfume bottle his mother had given Ann. "The glass was fragile," Ann said, "and he had tried all sorts of gentle methods to loosen the stopper, but none was effective. No hot water, rubber wrench, or rocking motion helped: the stopper held fast and we gave up."

Thirteen months after the death of Ann's father and mother, she moved into her first apartment. "All alone, an adult but still feeling like an orphan, I set up housekeeping. On my dresser was the unopenable perfume bottle."

Some months later, Ann awoke on a lazy Saturday morning. "I heard (sensed? felt?) my father tell me to go open the perfume bottle. I walked to the dresser without hesitation or doubt, picked up the bottle, and the stopper came out with one gentle turn. I cannot explain how, but I knew it would, and I knew it was he who made it so. I think it was a simple hello, a sweet way of saying, 'We're gone, but we haven't stopped watching over you.'"

Twenty years later, Ann's daughter, Lara, received a lovely garnet ring from her aunt. "It was more than just a present," Ann explained, "because my sister works very diligently to make up for my daughter's loss of grandparents. She really is aunt, grandmother and grandfather, all rolled into one. Lara really treasured the ring."

Shortly afterwards, returning from a wedding in another city, Lara lost the ring she cherished. Stopping at a fast-food hamburger restaurant, she used the rest room to change from wedding clothes into jeans. At home that night, putting away the clothes she had worn for the wedding she realized the ring was gone. "In moving the clothes from the restaurant bathroom to the trunk of the car," Ann said, "…it appeared that she had accidentally flung the ring from the car. We called the restaurant, and they checked the parking lot, but to no avail. Three of us checked and rechecked the trunk of the car, but no ring was found. It was a really sad loss."

Several months later, Ann had not thought about the ring for weeks. Reading the Sunday newspaper, "out of the blue my father told me again to do something. In words that were not spoken yet were clearly heard, he told me where the ring was. I went out to the car, opened the trunk, removed the carpet, removed the spare tire, removed the jack, and checked the nooks and crannies into which they all fit. There, shining and undamaged was the ring. I have never removed a spare tire or a jack from a trunk, but when I went to that car I knew exactly what I was looking for and exactly how to get to it. I *know* my father told me what to do."

Ann is puzzled that her father would help her with such "little stuff," but she knows such acts have been acts of love. "I wonder why he keeps coming back to this world when he has moved on to a much, much better place. It's one of the things I'm surely going to ask about when I see him again, though!"

# Reflection

## God Time

*Now and then,*
*here and there,*
*whispers of love*
*drift from the eternal realm*
*into this world of time and space.*
*If the stories in this book tell us anything,*
*they tell us this.*
*Whispers of love*
*drift from the hearts of those we love*
*who now live that better life called "eternal."*
*Mystifying as it may be sometimes*
*when these whispers of love come into our life,*
*there is no need to let these whispers bother or upset us.*
*For they are, after all, whispers of love*
*from which we may take comfort and encouragement.*
*They are whispers of love from those whose love for us*
*goes on and on,*
*on and on...*
*until we join them,*
*until we join them when the time is right,*
*in God's good time,*
*in that better life called "eternal."*

# EPILOGUE

## *A Rainbow From My Grandfather*

Gray clouds filled the central Oregon sky, and a cool spring breeze blew where it would as we gathered to bury the earthly remains of my grandfather. He had died three days before, after ninety-three years on the earth. A subdued cluster of some thirty people stood to one side of the flower-bedecked coffin, which was ready to be lowered into an open grave. No member of the clergy joined us in the small country cemetery. Instead, I, a thoroughly unordained person, read the prayers from the *Order of Christian Funerals*. A helpful priest had loaned me this liturgical-looking volume for the occasion and chided me as an "ersatz clergyman."

The day we received news of my grandfather's death, my mother was uncertain about what to do for a funeral service for her father. Even a generic Christian service in a funeral home presided over by a generic Protestant minister was, she decided, inappropriate. After all, Grandpa was never a churchgoing person. I guessed at what my mother was thinking and said, "Well, do you want me to do something?" To which she replied, "Yes." I'm the one in the family who committed formal theological studies....

I immediately realized that I hadn't the slightest idea what I was doing. On the one hand, I didn't want to misrepresent my grandfather's honest, if unspoken, stance toward life, the world, and other people. I didn't want to pretend he held religious perspectives he did not hold. On the other hand, I wanted to allow for the possibility of more overt forms of faith on the part of those in attendance. A balancing act, I decided, was my best bet.

As the sun alternately shone or hid behind clouds, I welcomed everyone, thanking them on behalf of our family for being there to honor "our father and grandfather, Walter." Admitting my inexperience at this sort of thing, which evoked encouraging smiles, I plunged ahead with "An Invitation to Prayer": "With faith in God, we must reverently bury our brother...."

Some of my fondest memories of my grandfather are of fishing trips we took together during the summers when I was in high school. All he did was take me fishing; he never delivered himself of any pearls of wisdom; he never tried to impress me with his skill as an angler. But he got more of a kick out of me catching a fish than if he himself hooked one.

I took from those good-humored times together the sense that Grandpa accepted me just as I was and enjoyed my company. I suppose he felt more free to adopt this uncritical attitude as a grandparent than he ever did as a parent. Yet he was, perhaps, reluctant to think of himself as a grandparent. Instead of "Grandpa," he always signed the occasional note or Christmas card, "G. P." I'm glad that a few years ago I wrote Grandpa a letter and thanked him for those fishing trips we shared.

It's no good trying to pin down the character of another person's relationship with the Creator. After the burial service was well and duly over, I was reminded of this rather forcefully. That evening, my mother handed me something she had found while going through her father's possessions. It was a baptismal certificate dated a few months after his birth in March of 1898 and signed by an Evangelical Lutheran Minister in Ava, Illinois. Written entirely in German, even Grandpa's name was spelled in the German way: "Walther."

My grandfather had saved his baptismal certificate all those decades, and sometime in the last few years he had come across it, and he put that certificate in a frame. Who knows what went through his mind and heart? Apparently, what his baptismal certificate stood for was important enough for him to take the trouble to frame it. After all, he could have thrown it away long ago.

I nodded to the man from the funeral home, who turned a lever, and as the coffin began its slow descent into the grave I read a series of intercessions to which the group responded, "Lord, have mercy."

Our intercessory prayers completed, Grandpa's body was now in its final resting place. I invited the immediate family to take a handful of earth and toss it into the grave. When I first thought of this gesture, I couldn't separate it in my mind from numerous Boot Hill burials in cowboy movies I had seen as a boy. My priest advisor had remarked, however, that it could be a gesture with much symbolic meaning.

My mother, my sister, and I dipped our hands into the newly dug, rich farmland soil, and we each dropped some down, down, onto my grandfather's coffin. It was an expression of love, as well as an act of farewell.

My part in Grandpa's graveside service required me to be a kind of liturgical leader as well as a mourner. Yet I found no conflict between the two roles. I was sorry to see my grandfather go, to be sure, but I found it impossible to feel sorry for him or to shed tears at his death. I look forward to seeing him again someday.

As I read the prayers I felt gratitude for the years I had known my grandfather and for the ways he helped me, with no conscious intention, to grow in self-acceptance and self-confidence when I was in my teens. I would say that I would like to do this or that, and he would respond with a barely concealed spirit of fun, "Oh, you would, would ya?" I can still hear his voice....

I invited anyone so inclined to speak a memory, anecdote, or personal comment about our father, grandfather, and friend, Walter. I primed the pump by recalling how my grandfather's handshake had always been so strong. Right up to the end of his life, when his body had grown weak and his memory unreliable, when he shook your hand you knew it had been shook.

A white-haired man in his seventies recalled how, over the years, he and Walt often teamed up in springtime to search cool, shaded places in the nearby mountains for edible wild mushrooms. Back they would come, gunny sacks heavy-laden, to fry fresh morrel mushrooms in butter and savor their taste by eating them slowly. He would miss those times, he said.

An old woman whispered her revelation to her middle-aged daughter, who reported that her mother happily recalled how helpful Walter had always been with customers in area grocery stores he managed or worked in for many years.

Others spoke up, too, with recollections of days gone by. Who could grieve long for the conclusion of such a life? Surely not I. One of God's greatest gifts to me had been a grandfather not inclined to church membership, but who had nothing but respect for my determination to attend Mass every Sunday morning.

I read a blessing for the grave: "O God, by whose mercy the faithful departed find rest, bless this grave, and send your holy angel to watch over it...."

A half-hour later, our purpose fulfilled and our visiting done, our three young sons were impatient to flee this place, impatient to be about living—and pizza for dinner. We drove slowly out of the old country cemetery, back to the two-lane highway. A twenty-minute drive would bring us to our motel room for the night.

The asphalt road sped through acre upon acre of newly plowed fields. A warm spring rain began to fall, so I switched on our mini-van's windshield wipers. In the distance, however, the late afternoon sun fell upon the fields through patches of clear blue sky.

Then, as I drove, I glanced to my left and beheld the most perfect rainbow I have ever seen. "Look!" I exclaimed to my wife, our three sons and my mother. "A rainbow!" The rainbow towered into the sky, was visible in its entirety, end to end, and all its colors were vivid. I couldn't help myself. Disregarding the tug of skepticism, I took this as an epistle from my grandfather, a word of hope and promise, as the rainbow was for Noah after the deluge.

All is well, said the shimmering, colorful, mile-high rainbow from my grandfather; all is well, and all manner of thing shall be well.

# EPIGRAM

"God is so good,
just spinning out love all around me,
allowing me to keep meeting beautiful people.
All living is love, you know.
Joy is helping others."

–ELLA MILLER, *OF OAKTON, VIRGINIA, ON THE OCCASION OF HER
114TH BIRTHDAY, DECEMBER 6, 1994, IN AN INTERVIEW WITH
WASHINGTON POST COLUMNIST COURTLAND MILLOY*